THE WESTHILL PROJECT R.E. 5–16

JUDAISM

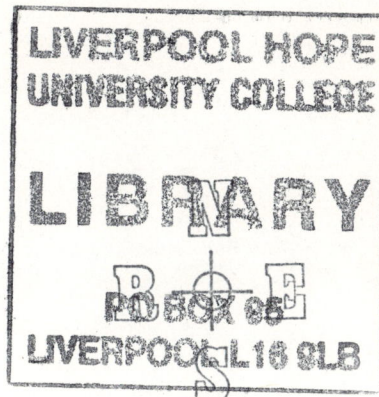

TEACHER'S MANUAL

Stanley Thornes Publishers (Ltd)

Sarah Montagu

Series editors John Rudge
Garth Read
Geoff Teece

First published in 1990 by:
Stanley Thornes (Publishers) Ltd
Old Station Drive
Leckhampton
CHELTENHAM GL53 0DN
England

British Library Cataloguing in Publication Data

Judaism.
    Teacher's manual
    1. Judaism
    I. Montagu, Sarah   II. Series
    296

    ISBN 1-871402-23-9

Typeset by Tech-Set, Gateshead, Tyne & Wear
Printed and bound in Great Britain by Ebenezer Baylis & Son Limited, Worcester

Acknowledgements
Two trust funds have contributed in important ways to the production of all the materials which
make up the Jewish strand within the Westhill Project R.E. 5–16. St Peter's Saltley Trust made a
grant to the Regional R.E. Centre in Westhill College and the Anne Frank Fonds (Switzerland)
made a grant to the Centre for the Study of Judaism and Jewish/Christian Relations in the Selly
Oak College. These two grants enabled Sarah Montagu to share time between the two Centres. In
relation to this project, Sarah has contributed in the capacity of author and consultant. The authors,
editors and publishers are grateful for these generous grants.

Members of the Centre for the Study of Judaism and Jewish/Christian Relations in Selly Oak,
Birmingham, have also acted as consultants in the making of this book.

Margaret Breiner, Ceri Greves and Peter Woodward contributed to the writing of the teaching
scheme on pages 56 ff.

All quotations from the Hebrew Bible are taken from *Tanakh*, published by the Jewish Publication
Society, 1985
All quotations from rabbinic writings are taken from *A Rabbinic Anthology*, by Claude Montefiore
and Herbert Loewe, published by Schocken, 1975.
All quotations from the liturgy are taken from *The Authorised Daily Prayer Book*, published by Eyre
and Spottiswode, 1962.

Contents

General introduction

The Westhill Project is produced by the Regional R.E. Centre (Midlands). It is designed to produce a comprehensive package of materials related to the teaching of Religious Education in schools.

There are several different sets of materials in this package. While they are interrelated, each set serves a particular purpose in relation to the teaching of R.E. from the early years, through primary and secondary schooling and into teacher education.

Teacher's materials

How do I teach R.E.? is the teacher's manual for the whole project. It sets out to explore the structure of the school subject, R.E., and to show how the general aim of the subject can be translated into classroom practice. It is concerned with the question 'How to teach R.E.?' as much as it is with the questions 'What to teach?' and 'Why teach it?'. Thus it provides a foundation text for use by students in their initial teacher training and presents to serving teachers a set of clear guidelines for school-based curriculum development in regard to this subject.

In the book *How do I teach R.E.?* the claim is made that R.E. can, and should, be taught through the use of two different (though equally valid and effective) approaches. One is called the **Systems approach** and the other is called the **Life Themes approach.** There is a manual for each of the faith systems, offering a comprehensive overview of that world religion.

The Life Themes teaching materials are accompanied by full teaching support at the appropriate level: for example, the manual *Life themes in the early years* accompanies the picture packs for primary schools (see below).

Each of the supplementary manuals includes an extensive teaching scheme which shows how the material contained in these manuals can be taught in a developmental way from the earliest years through to the upper secondary years.

Pupil's materials

Within the Westhill Project package there are also three different sets of teaching materials which may be used directly with pupils. These materials embody the principles and content outlined in the teacher's manuals.

(i) *Pupil's books – Systems*
Four pupil's books, designed for use with children in junior and secondary schools, accompany each of the supplementary teacher's manuals on the world religions. These follow the teaching schemes set out in the supplementary manuals and relate to four broad bands of schooling.

Book 1 – Lower juniors 7–8 years)
Book 2 – Upper juniors (9–11 years)
Book 3 – Lower secondary (12–14 years)
Book 4 – Upper secondary (15–16+ years)

(ii) *Photopacks – Systems*
Each pack of 20 A3 colour photographs relates to one of the supplementary manuals. These pictures illustrate aspects of each religion or a significant life theme, as expressed in four different contexts: family life, religious community life, personal life and public life. Detailed information is printed on the back of each picture under three headings: *description* of the event photographed; *significance* within the religion as a whole; *beliefs* being expressed.

(iii) *Picture packs – Life Themes*
There are three separate large-format picture packs in this set of materials, each containing 20 pictures designed primarily for use when teaching R.E. according to the Life Themes approach to children in their early years. These packs contain full-colour artist's drawings and original photographs relating to six of the categories of life themes outlined in the two teacher's manuals *How do I teach R.E.?* (p.21) and *Life themes in the early years.*

Most of the material in this package stems from an ongoing dialogue between classroom teachers and authors in the context of in-service courses over a number of years. Where particular teachers have contributed directly to the material, this is duly acknowledged.

As an exercise in curriculum development this scheme makes no pretence to being definitive. It is intended to contribute to the development of the subject. The authors and publishers would therefore warmly welcome both comment and criticism, as well as further examples of good practical work in R.E. which could be considered for inclusion in the overall scheme.

Series introduction

The manuals in this series are part of a comprehensive package of materials, produced by the staff of the Regional R.E. Centre (Midlands) for use by R.E. teachers in both primary and secondary schools. While each of six supplementary manuals relates to a particular world religion they are not comprehensive text books on those religions. There are countless volumes of such books, written from a variety of perspectives, for example, historical, theological, sociological, devotional and polemical. These manuals are written with a strictly educational purpose in mind. They are written from the perspective of the curriculum and teaching requirements of a multi-faith R.E. programme in primary and secondary schools.

Nonetheless, it is important to know that the sections describing the particular religion in each book of the series have been written by practising members of that religion. It is intended that the religious beliefs and practices are described clearly, authentically and without apology, and yet without any assumptions being made or implied about the reader's acceptance or rejection of the religion now or in the future. The teaching scheme at the end of each book in this series has been developed by staff of the Regional R.E. Centre in co-operation with practising teachers.

Objectives

Each of these manuals has four quite specific objectives in relation to a particular world religion and to those significant areas of shared human experience to which religions address themselves in one form or another.

1 To provide teachers with an overview of the world religion, in this case Judaism, in its contemporary forms.
2 To organise and present the material in a way that makes it available and teachable in both primary and secondary schools.
3 To indicate a structure, along with example units of work, which encourages a progressive development of the subject for children across the 7–16 age range.
4 To help teachers adopt a language style which, while remaining faithful to the religion, does not make any assumptions about the beliefs of any of the participants in the class.

Religion and frogs!

Of course there is a sense in which the exercise of analysing a religion in terms of its component parts results in distortion, if not destruction of the real thing. Very few practising religious people think of their faith in terms of a collection of interrelated beliefs, spiritual values and practices. For them it is a living whole and its power and beauty permeate their life. Nevertheless, analytical dissection is important, useful and perhaps necessary for the purposes of education in schools.

R.E. is not the only school subject dependent on this kind of activity for teaching purposes. The teacher of biology may well require students to dissect, say, a frog. This dissection may be seen as valuable and even essential for the advancement of knowledge, understanding and even the care and protection of frogs. However, in its dissected form the frog is no longer a frog. It is equally important, therefore, that pupils are given opportunities to see living frogs in all their splendour of colour, form and efficiency in the context of their natural habitat. This is relatively easy with frogs. It is extremely difficult with religion. Religion is not contained in any one simple form or expression. Its essential character transcends the observable phenomena and may never be totally accessible to the majority of children in schools.

An honest awareness of this situation, however, does not negate the value of the exercise in relation to religion any more than it does for frogs. The analytical exercise, for all its limitations, is still one of the tools which people use in their search for truth and understanding. Whatever else schools exist for, they certainly exist to promote respect for and increase skill in the use of this tool in relation to important areas of human endeavour and experience. The contention here is that religion and the formation of each child's individual pattern of belief are very important areas of endeavour and experience and schools have a necessary and important role to play in advancing knowledge and understanding of them.

If the idea of dissecting Judaism is unappealing, we could change the image and suggest that this manual provides the teacher with a number of different perspectives from which to view this complex and many-faceted religion. Either way, the intention and hope is that specialist and non-specialist teachers, in both primary and secondary schools, will find here a ready reference book when they come to prepare R.E. lessons which draw material from this particular world religion.

Transliteration of Hebrew words

Hebrew uses its own alphabet and must therefore be transliterated into the Roman alphabet. The Hebrew alphabet has 22 consonants and 9 vowels, for some of which there is no exact equivalent in the Roman alphabet. There is also no universally accepted system of transliteration, so the conventions adopted here may differ from those used in other books. The main points to note are the use of *ḥ, kh, k* and *ḳ. Ḥ* and *kh* are gutturals pronounced rather like 'ch' in the Scottish 'loch', although *ḥ* is pronounced rather further back in the throat. *Ḳ* is the non-aspirated form of *kh,* so *ḳ* is used to denote a similar sounding Hebrew letter, to distinguish between the two. This means that words such as *Ḳiddush* or *tiḳḳun* may be found as *Kiddush* or *tikkun* in other books. The other letters for which there are no equivalents in the Roman alphabet are the silent consonants *alef* and *ayin.* These are transliterated as ' and ' respectively.

A further problem is pronunciation, which differs among Hebrew speakers. We have used the Sefardi pronunciation commonly used in Modern Hebrew, whereas other books may use the Ashkenazi pronunciation. Examples of this would be *kosher* for *kasher* and *Shabbes* for *Shabbat.* Most Hebrew words in the Sefardi pronunciation are accented on the last syllable.

PART ONE

Judaism: a world religion

What is Judaism?

Within the context of multi-faith R.E., Judaism can be presented as one world religion among many. Some particular aspects may also have to be taken into account, for instance the question of whether Judaism is a race, a religion or a culture. In general, however, Judaism shares many characteristics and the same basic structural form with all other religions. In other words, it consists of a central core of beliefs and a particular form of spirituality which provide the background and motivation for a wide range of practices and moral and ethical values. This central core also provides a framework by which the Jewish understanding of humanity's position and function on earth, and the particular task of the Jewish people, may be understood.

JUDAISM

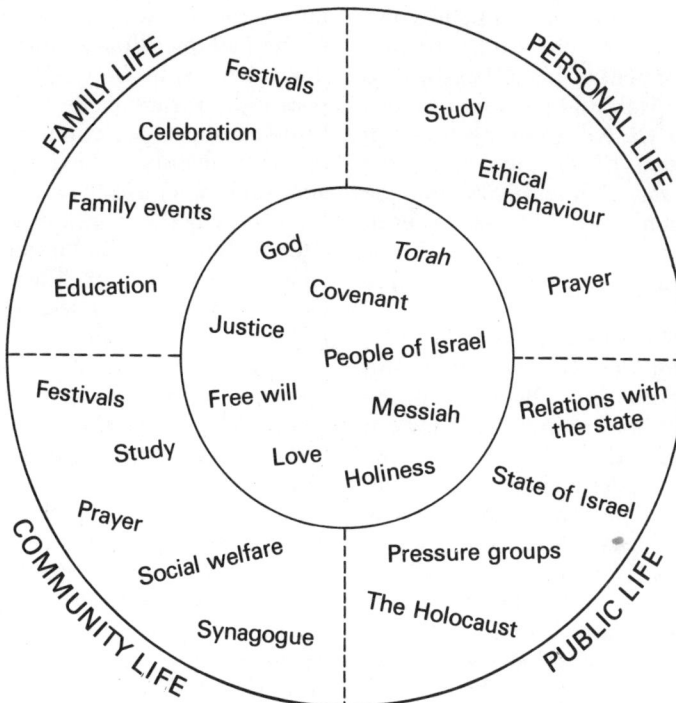

The attempt to describe Judaism as a world religion is a difficult but necessary task for teachers of R.E. They must present it in a way which is faithful to the essential character of the religion – a particularly delicate job for those who come from other traditions and whose knowledge is derived mainly from books. They must be able to take into account those elements which unite all Jews, but at the same time reflect the diversity of Judaism's different strands of tradition.

The diagrammatic model offered on page 1 presents an overview of Judaism and in the following chapters the salient features will be examined and explained.

The inner circle identifies some of the key beliefs and concepts which characterise Judaism and are central to an understanding of the basis of the Jewish faith. As will be seen, there may be very different views on what is to be understood under each of these headings and therefore differences in how they are expressed in the religious life of the individual Jew. Nevertheless, these concepts are those to which almost every Jew will refer when asked to explain Judaism. Obviously, each concept chosen here also covers a large range of sub-concepts, some of which could be examined under more than one heading. The third section of this manual will deal with these concepts in some detail.

Words in the outer segments identify some of the characteristic forms of religious expression found in Judaism, based on its central beliefs and spirituality. It is important to note that the broken lines between each segment suggest that they do not indicate discrete, watertight compartments. Many of the practices we will examine occur in more than one context of people's lives; for instance, aspects of personal or family life may be celebrated by the community. The size of each segment should also not necessarily be taken to represent the relative importance of any one area of life.

Pupils will be able to relate to some or all of the four contexts. They can identify experiences and practices that occur in their own lives and in the lives of their families or their community. They can then be helped to see how different behaviour can result from holding different beliefs or from belonging to different communities. There will, of course, be some inevitable repetition as a result of organising material under contextual headings. For instance, the Sabbath is marked by activities in most of the four contexts and it is important to understand the pivotal position the day holds in Jewish life. In presenting material on the Sabbath to pupils, teachers must find an appropriate sequence which avoids unnecessary repetition and achieves at least the following objectives:

- Pupils gain a comprehensive knowledge of the importance of the Sabbath in Jewish life.
- They are able to identify ways in which the Sabbath is celebrated by the individual, the family and the community.
- They can identify ways in which their own lifestyles may reflect some of these Jewish practices.

There will be occasions when the teacher will want to focus on the theme 'Shabbat' and on the day as a whole. At other times, the theme of 'Jewish family life' will contain references to the way in which the Sabbath affects the pattern of family life. Most of the themes in this book can be approached from different aspects and the structure adopted here is not intended to be prescriptive.

Unity within Judaism

Most Jews, regardless of their religious outlook, feel themselves to be inextricably linked to the Jewish people. There are several factors which contribute towards this feeling of identity and unity, and these should be borne in mind when trying to understand Judaism.

The history of the Jewish people is very important both for the Jew and for Judaism. Much of the Hebrew Bible is an attempt to understand the relationship between God and the Jewish people by means of its history and many of the Jewish festivals are connected in some way with historical events. A Jewish child's education will almost always include something of the history of Judaism, whether through study of the Bible and later writings, tales of famous personalities of the past or the history of different Jewish communities. The events which led to the Jewish nationalist movement of Zionism in the 19th century and the eventual foundation of the state of Israel in 1948 give a modern focus to this historical sense. Obviously, it is impossible in a manual of this kind to try and give a history of Judaism but the teacher of R.E. is strongly recommended to read some of the books on the subject in order to understand this aspect of Jewish consciousness. The bibliography at the end of this manual includes some suggestions for further reading.

The Hebrew language is another unifying factor between Jews of all religious persuasions. Although the majority of Jews probably have some other language as their first tongue, Hebrew has been the language of prayer and of study throughout the centuries and is always a vital part of the education of the Jewish child. The revival of Hebrew as a spoken vernacular at the end of the 19th century and its adoption as the language of the land of Israel was a powerful impetus against the forces of linguistic assimilation. Even Liberal and Reform Jews, who include prayers and readings in the vernacular in their services, have many prayers in Hebrew and teach it in their religion schools.

Persecution is also, sadly, another factor that binds Jews together. Obviously, the history of the Jews contains many periods of peace, intellectual activity and prosperity. However, between these periods, there have been events of horrific persecution as well as times of discrimination and oppression. The most recent and most over-whelming of these was the Holocaust, the programme of mass murder carried out by the Nazis in central and eastern Europe during the Second World War. Such events have often, paradoxically, ensured Jewish survival by fostering a spirit of defiance and identity with the Jewish people. Most Jews, without having a persecution complex, have an awareness of the significance of such events for them. It is important for the R.E. teacher to have some idea of what the Holocaust and other persecutions mean to the Jew.

Diversity within Judaism

Teachers should bear in mind from the outset that there is considerable variety, within Judaism, of religious attitudes and cultural background.

Sometimes it is as a result of geographical and cultural differences. Since the time of the destruction of the First Temple in 586 B.C.E. and the Babylonian Exile (2 Kings 25), there have been Jewish communities in all parts of the world and each community has developed individual patterns of celebration and custom. The two major groupings are the Sefardi and the Ashkenazi Jews. *Sefarad* and *Ashkenaz* are Hebrew names of countries in the Bible that in later tradition came to be applied to Spain and Germany respectively. The Sefardi Jews are communities that follow Mediterranean and Eastern Jewish customs and Ashkenazi Jews follow the customs of Northern, Eastern and Central Europe. Each group also has its own vernacular, although these are less widely used now than they used to be. Ashkenazi Jews spoke Yiddish, a form of Middle High German

with some Russian or Slovak and Hebrew terms, and Sefardi Jews spoke Ladino, a form of Spanish. Both languages are written in Hebrew characters. There are also other smaller but distinctive communities, for instance the Falashas of Ethiopia and Benei Israel of India. The differences evince themselves mainly in customs concerning food, tunes used in prayer at home and in the synagogue, names given to children and so on, rather than in major ideological conflict. There is little animosity between such groups, although they tend to maintain their particular customs even when they migrate to other countries and live in cities with communities of Jews of different geographical origins. An example of this process at work is to be found in Jerusalem, where there are many synagogues which are identified by the geographical origin of the particular community and where differences of liturgy and custom are maintained.

Ideological differences cause more tension and there are several distinctive tendencies within Judaism. In the 19th century, particularly in Germany, there was a movement to reform the Jewish religion in the wake of the Enlightenment and the new critical attitude towards the text of the Bible. Reform Judaism did not accept that the text of the Bible as it now stands is the direct revelation of God as transmitted to Moses on Mount Sinai and still less did it accept the interpretations and rulings of the rabbis which are contained in the *Mishnah* and *Talmud* as authoritative and as an element of the Sinaitic revelation. This attitude obviously had enormous implications for the belief and practice of Judaism. In general, Reform Judaism made a distinction between the ethical commands of Judaism, which are for all time, and the rituals, which are subject to change in different ages and societies. It gave the individual conscience the last word in determining practice, and many elements of traditional Judaism were 'modernised' or played down. The first reformers were often very radical and modern Reform Judaism has in many cases returned to more traditional rabbinic interpretations, more use of Hebrew or greater emphasis on the role of the land of Israel. In England, another movement, known as Liberal Judaism, was founded in 1902. Liberal Judaism is in general less traditional than Reform but the two movements share many characteristics and the rabbis for both are trained at the same institution.

In America, there are several different move-ments. The Reform movement there is probably more akin to the English Liberal movement. The middle ground is occupied by the Conservative movement which was also started at the turn of the century. Conservative Judaism emphasises both the historical evolution of Judaism and the value of traditional practice. Although they share the non-fundamentalist attitude of other non-traditional Jews, they give the traditional *Halakhah* (Jewish law) a greater voice. They therefore observe many of the commandments that Reform Jews do not. It is numerically much the most important segment of the American Jewish population and probably owes its popularity to the course it steers between the radicalism of Reform and the ideological demands of Orthodoxy. There are a few Conservative synagogues in Britain, mostly in London; the British branch of the movement is called *Masorti*, traditional.

Reconstructionism is another American movement and although small in numbers, has had a disproportionate effect on Jewish life there. It was started in the 1920s and is based almost entirely on the religious thought of its main leader, Mordecai Kaplan. He developed a theology which defines God as a 'power or process that works for human salvation or self-fulfilment'. He therefore rejected the traditional ideas of divine revelation but because he also emphasised the value of traditional Jewish 'folkways', Reconstructionist Jews often observe many of the ritual commandments as part of their commitment to Jewish culture.

The term Orthodox was first applied to traditional Judaism to distinguish it from Reform. Orthodox Judaism is in essence fundamentalist – it accepts the divine nature of revelation and accords the traditional rabbinic interpretations of the Bible full authority in determining practice. Orthodoxy itself has, however, reacted to the demands of modern life and there are different tendencies within it. The neo- or modern Orthodox movement follows the ideas of Samson Raphael Hirsch, a rabbi of the late 19th century, who claimed that it was possible both to be a fully Orthodox Jew and to participate in Western civilisation, to allow *Torah* to illuminate the best that Western science and philosophy can offer and vice versa. There are

also ultra-Orthodox communities, such as the various Hasidic groups, which tend to be more inward looking and whose patterns of practice and culture are very distinctive. The majority of Jews in Britain belong to Orthodox synagogues although they may not all follow a strictly Orthodox level of practice. In this manual, we have taken as our starting point the beliefs and practices of Orthodoxy, and, wherever possible, the variations found in non-traditional Judaism have been noted.

All these groups differ from each other in terms of ideology and practice, and there is sometimes tension and even animosity between them, particularly in Israel. It must be noted, however, that movement between each group is perfectly possible. A phenomenon of recent years is the *Ba'al Teshuvah*, a returner or penitent. This is the term applied to a Jew of non-traditional background who has returned to Orthodox belief and practice. Equally, members of an Orthodox synagogue may choose to join a Reform synagogue.

To convey something of the flavour of this complex religion within the context of a multi-faith R.E. programme is a challenging task for teachers. It is a particularly challenging task for teachers brought up and educated in a traditionally Christian country. Judaism has in the past sometimes been taught in a way that does it less than full justice and teachers often have to free themselves of misconceptions. The two most damaging assumptions are that Judaism is the religion of the Old Testament, a view which ignores the last 2000 years of lively and important development, and that Judaism is an incomplete religion, a view which sees it as an adjunct of Christianity.

The book *How do I teach R.E.?*, of which this manual is a supplement, provides a detailed discussion of how to develop and teach a multi-faith programme. The aim here is to examine the Jewish religion closely, to show it as a valid, living tradition, and to identify some of the ways in which it can be presented in R.E. lessons for children in both primary and secondary schools.

PART TWO

Jewish beliefs

Judaism may seem to many to be a religion of action, expressed in a particular way of living. Underlying it and fundamental to its practice is, however, a range of basic beliefs and concepts. Obviously, all Jews do not share these beliefs in the same way, nor may they see them all as being equally important. Judaism is not, on the whole, a dogmatic religion and although there have been various formulations of belief throughout its history, these have never been accepted as official creeds and their acceptance has generally been implicit rather than explicit. The nature of traditional rabbinic debate, where paradoxes are set up or two opposing views are presented side by side, tends to result in open-ended statements and this is reflected in many discussions of belief. Some of the concepts that we will be discussing here might be emphasised by one group in Judaism more than another but each one is vital for an understanding of the values and practices that go to make up Judaism and will provide a useful key to the exploration of the Jewish religion.

We shall be exploring the following concepts and beliefs:

God

Brit or Covenant

Torah or Revelation

Mitzvah or Commandment

'*Am Yisra'el* or the people of Israel

Free will and the nature of humanity

Teshuvah or Repentance

Messiah and Redemption

God

Introduction

Judaism is a religion of enormous complexity and diversity and, as we have already stated, one can find a very wide variety of statements of belief. The element that unites all the possible variations of Jewish faith is the belief in one God. This God is the creator and sustainer of the universe, the only being whose existence is necessary, uncaused and eternal, on whom all other beings depend. God transcends the world, yet 'the whole earth is full of his glory' (Isaiah 6:3). God is a personal deity whom humanity can love with the highest and most complete love. Equally, God loves humanity and is involved in human history and destiny. God is absolutely one and unique so that no other existing thing can be compared with God in any way.

Rabbinic theology

The theology of the rabbis, who, from about 50 B.C.E. to about 500 C.E. set down the traditions and interpretations of *Torah* on which modern Judaism is based, is often presented as a series of paradoxes. God is both transcendent and immanent, transcendent as the creator who is above and beyond all that which is created and immanent as the *Shekhinah,* the close presence that is accessible to all. This view strikes a balance between the deist position, that God is utterly distant from creation and humankind, and the pantheist position, that God and nature are one. God is infinite and all-powerful but listens to humanity's prayers and protects and preserves them. God's greatness is made manifest in the wonders of creation.

JEWISH BELIEFS ABOUT GOD

From *Torah*

*Hear, O Israel! The Lord is our God,
the Lord alone. You shall love the Lord your
God with all your heart and with all your soul
and with all your might. Take to heart these
instructions with which I charge you this day.
Impress them upon your children. Recite them
when you stay at home and when you are
away, when you lie down and when you get
up. Bind them as a sign on your hand and let
them serve as a symbol on your forehead;
inscribe them on the doorposts of your house
and on your gates.*

(Deuteronomy 6: 4–9)

From the Writings

*O Lord, you have examined me and known me.
When I sit down or stand up you know it;
you discern my thoughts from afar.
You observe my walking and my reclining,
and are familiar with all my ways.
There is not a word on my tongue but that you,
O Lord, know it well.
You hedge me before and behind;
you lay your hand upon me.
It is beyond my knowledge; it is a mystery;
I cannot fathom it.
Where can I escape from your spirit?
Where can I flee from your presence?
If I ascend to heaven, you are there;
if I descend to Sheol*, you are there too.
If I take wing with the dawn to come to rest
on the western horizon, even there your hand
will be guiding me, your right hand be
holding me fast.
If I say, 'Surely darkness will conceal me, night
will provide me with cover,'
Darkness is not dark for you; night is as light
as day; darkness and light are the same.
It was you who created my conscience;
you fashioned me in my mother's womb.
I praise you, for I am awesomely,
wondrously made; your work is wonderful;
I know it very well.*

(Psalm 139: 1–14)

*The abode of the dead

From rabbinical writings

*Rabbi Johanan said: Thirteen kinds of mercy
are written in the scriptures about God.
'The Lord (1), the Lord (2), God (3), merciful
(4), gracious (5), longsuffering (6), abundant
in loving-kindness (7) and fidelity (8), keeping
mercy to a thousand generations (9), forgiving
iniquity (10), transgressions (11) and sin (12)
and acquitting (13)'.*

(Pesiḳta Kahana 57a on Exodus 34: 6–7)

(Each of God's names used in this
passage is taken in the exegesis to refer
to a different aspect of God's mercy).

From the liturgy

*Blessed are You, Lord our God, King of the
Universe who forms light and creates darkness,
who makes peace and creates all things. In
mercy you give light to the earth and to those
who dwell on it, and in your goodness, you
renew the work of creation each day
continually. How numerous are your works,
O Lord! In wisdom have you made them all:
the earth is full of your possessions. O King,
alone exalted from aforetime, praised, glorified
and extolled from days of old; O eternal God, in
your abundant mercies have mercy on us, Lord
of our strength, Rock of our refuge, Shield of
our salvation, Refuge of ours!
The blessed God, whose knowledge is great,
prepared and made the sun's rays: he has
formed a good which brings glory to his name.
He set the heavenly luminaries round about his
strength. The chiefs of his host are holy beings
who exalt the Almighty and continually declare
the glory of God and his holiness. Be blessed,
O Lord our God, for the excellence of your
handiwork, and for the bright luminaries which
you have made that they should glorify you.*

(from the morning prayers)

Humanity can know something of the deeds of God through history, both on the microcosmic level, for instance in the yearly renewal of the seasons, and on the macrocosmic level, for instance in the revelation at Mount Sinai. People can approach God through prayer, devotion and by doing God's will as expressed in the commandments of *Torah*. However, neither knowledge of God's deeds nor human approach to God can give insight into the inner being of God.

Jewish philosophy

The Jewish philosophers of the Middle Ages, such as Maimonides, approached questions about the nature of God and God's relation with humanity in a much more systematic way than the earlier rabbis. They emphasised far more the transcendence, the absolute otherness of God, though they did not deny that God cares for and is involved with humanity. They grappled with the problems of what can be said about God, if you accept that to use human imagery or to ascribe human attributes and emotions is to limit God. They also examined Bible passages which use anthropomorphic terms such as God's hand, God's mighty arm and so on, in a more questioning light.

Mystical theology

The Jewish mystical tradition, known as the *Kabbalah* or received tradition, developed a distinctive theology. It is too complex a system to do more than indicate some of its major themes here, so it is recommended that teachers read some of the specialist books on the topic.

The *Kabbalah* emphasises the complete otherness of God. God is called *'En Sof,* the limitless one, and nothing of God's nature can be known or understood by humanity. The only way in which we can perceive God is in the manifestations or emanations of God which flow from the infinite God and through which the finite world is created. These emanations are reckoned to be 10 in number and each reflects a different aspect of God. The *Kabbalah* devotes much attention to the relationship between the *'En Sof* and the emanations or *Sefirot.*

Another kabbalistic idea deals with the relationship between God and creation. Although the created world is finite and temporal, it was created through a divine manifestation and everything in this lower realm is paralleled by an element of the perfect upper realm. As Gershom Scholem puts it

'Creation is nothing but an external development of those forces which are active and alive in God himself.'[1] Not only are all elements of creation a reflection of a divine reality but they are all intimately and inextricably linked with it so that there is a constant flow of divine energy into the world and God's light fills all creation. This relationship is a mutual one, and one of the *Kabbalah's* most radical ideas is that human actions can affect the flow of divine power. Creation and, more particularly, the fall of *'adam,* brought a disunity into the previously completely unified emanations. Every time a human being fulfills a *mitzvah* (a commandment), a temporary reunification occurs which permits a greater flow of divine energy. This reinterpretation of the significance of religious and moral action is one of the *Kabbalah's* most important contributions.

Contemporary theology

One of the major themes in modern Jewish theology is the response to the Holocaust in which 6,000,000 Jews were murdered systematically by Adolf Hitler's Nazi regime in Europe during the Second World War. For many Jewish writers, the Holocaust has demanded a complete rethinking of theology. A minority have concluded that God is dead after Auschwitz, that it is impossible to conceive of a God who could have 'allowed' something like the Holocaust to happen. Others have seen the Holocaust as the most terrible example of the evil that human beings can inflict on each other and have concluded that if humanity is to have free will, it must have the free will to choose evil as well as good. If the Jew denies God as a result of the Holocaust, it is a denial also of everything that the 6,000,000 victims died for and, in the words of Emil Fackenheim, one of the best known Holocaust theologians, 'allows Hitler to have the last word'.[2]

Another theme of contemporary Jewish theology that has come to the forefront since the founding of the state of Israel is the theology of power, the implications for Judaism of being in a position of control. Independent Jewish statehood had already ceased to exist by the time of the formative period of Jewish law. Although the major works of this period, the *Mishnah* and the *Talmud,* often refer to the time when a sovereign Jewish state existed, the rabbis were well aware

[1] From *Major Trends in Jewish Mysticism,* Schocken, New York, 1965

[2] From *God's Presence in History,* Harper Torchbooks, New York, 1972

that they were describing an ideal, rather than an actual state of affairs. The history of Judaism has meant that Jews have lived as a subject nation in many different countries from that time till 1948. The challenges of the modern state of Israel have social and political, but also profound theological implications, with which the theology of power attempts to come to grips.

Relationship to shared human experience

Jewish ideas about God reflect some of the responses of humanity when faced with the wonders and mysteries of creation and their own place within it. For those who find scientific explanations of how the universe began inadequate, and who cannot accept that all the complex and mutually dependent forms of life came about purely by accident, the idea of a creator and sustainer of the universe provides an answer.

The idea that the earth and everything in it belong ultimately to God and not to humanity gives further motivation to those who feel that people have a responsibility not only to themselves but also to the rest of humanity, both now and in the future, and that they should act as caretakers and stewards rather than as owners.

From Jewish images of God and God's role as creator and sustainer of the universe follows the belief that God makes demands on us. Humanity tends to search for a general moral framework within which life can be conducted. For Jews the ethical and moral values of the religion are the necessary response to belief in God. Judaism is sometimes referred to as a religion of ethical monotheism; that is to say, belief in God is empty without ethical behaviour, and ethical behaviour is meaningless without belief in God.

Belief in God can also provide reassurance and help humanity to find some meaning in the mystery of life and the universe. Ideas of a loving God and of what God wants us to do can provide direction and a realisation of the significance of every human action. They can also provide a focus for the human need to express praise and gratitude for our lives and everything in them.

Brit or covenant

Introduction

All the various covenants found in the *Torah* have a common pattern. They involve a two-sided pact or promise: God enters into a relationship marked by certain mutual obligations with an individual or a group. The covenant, or *Brit*, is often also marked with a special sign: the covenant with Noah with a rainbow, the covenant with Abraham with the ceremony of circumcision, the covenant at Mount Sinai with the *Torah*. Each covenant marks a particular stage in the historical relationship of God with humanity in general and the Jewish people in particular.

The covenant with Noah

The covenant with Noah, in Jewish understanding, marks the establishment of a particular relationship between God and all of humanity. It reflects Jewish ideas about the nature of God, the fact that God is intimately involved with the created world. It is also the beginning of a process by which God gradually reveals more and more of humanity's task in that world. In this particular case, God's promise is to bless humanity and never again to destroy it by flood. Humanity's reciprocal obligation is to begin work as God's partner in caring for and tending the created world, by following God's precepts of justice.

In later Jewish teaching, the standards of behaviour set for Noah and his sons become the minimum requirement for non-Jews. Jews are obliged to keep the commandments revealed as a result of the Sinaitic covenant in order to earn their share of salvation. Non-Jews are obliged to keep what are known as the 'Seven Commandments of Noah' in order to earn salvation – to have one God, not to blaspheme God, not to commit adultery, not to steal, not to murder, to practise justice and to be kind to animals. This teaching of Judaism is one reason why Judaism is not a strongly missionary religion – it it not a prerequisite for salvation to have followed the particular path of Judaism.

The covenant with the Patriarchs (Abraham, Isaac and Jacob) and at Sinai

These covenants mark the beginning of God's relationship with the Jewish people. God's promise is to bless the Jewish people and to maintain a close relationship with them for all time. Israel's task is to follow the words of the *Torah*, the sign of the covenant at Mount Sinai. This task is expressed in the patriarchal covenant with the words 'to keep the way of the Lord by doing what is just and right' (Genesis 18: 19) and in the

THE CONCEPT OF COVENANT

From *Torah*

When Abram was ninety-nine years old, the Lord appeared to Abram and said to him, 'I am El Shaddai. Walk in my ways and be blameless. I will establish my covenant between me and you, and I will make you exceedingly numerous. Abram threw himself on his face; and God spoke to him further, 'As for me, this is my covenant with you: you shall be the father of a multitude of nations . . . I will maintain my covenant between me and you and your offspring to come, as an everlasting covenant through the ages, to be God to you and to your offspring to come. I give the land you sojourn in to you and your offspring to come, all the land of Canaan, as an everlasting possession. I will be their God.'

(Genesis 17: 1–21)

Moses went up to God. The Lord called to him from the mountain, saying, 'Thus shall you say to the house of Jacob and declare to the children of Israel: "You have seen what I did to the Egyptians, how I bore you on eagles' wings and brought you to me. Now then, if you will obey me faithfully and keep my covenant, you shall be my treasured possession among all the peoples. Indeed, all the earth is mine, but you shall be to me a kingdom of priests and a holy nation".'

(Exodus 19: 3–6)

From the Writings

This shall be my covenant with them, said the Lord: My spirit which is upon you and the words which I have placed in your mouth, shall not be absent from your mouth, nor from the mouth of your children, nor from the mouth of your children's children – said the Lord – from now on, for all time.

(Isaiah 59: 21)

Sinaitical covenant by the words 'you shall be to me a kingdom of priests and a holy nation'. Israel must bear witness to God's existence and nature by following the commandments of righteousness and by also living a life of a particular pattern and discipline, a holy life.

The covenant in later Jewish teaching

The theme of the covenant became central to Jewish teaching about Israel's role in the world. God's eternal faithfulness to the covenant and Israel's continual backsliding is one of the most often recurring refrains of prophetical and rabbinic writing. The covenant between God and the Jewish people expresses ideas about their relationship and about the particular responsibilities that devolve on the Jewish people as a result of the covenant.

Relationship to shared human experience

As we have seen in the section on belief in God, Judaism emphasises that God is intimately involved in creation and particularly in human destiny, even though God is infinitely greater than creation. Ideas about the covenant make the relationship between God and humanity explicit and provide a focus for human feelings about the relationship.

Each covenant is a mutual pact between two parties. Jewish beliefs about God's side of all of the covenants, that God promises to protect and stay close to all humanity, and to have a particular relationship with the Jewish people, provide reassurance and a reminder of God's faithfulness. The human side, that we have certain responsiblities and roles as God's covenant partners, elevates the significance of human action to an extraordinarily high level.

The covenants offer a response to the human need to make sense out of life and the quest for security and certainty in a perplexing world.

Torah

Introduction

The Torah is, for the Jews, the concrete evidence for God's relationship with them. It contains accounts of how God has been involved with them in history and also, more importantly, God's instructions for the way in which God wants them to live. The word torah actually means instruction

or teaching, this is the most important function of revelation.

The narrow definition of Torah is the first five books of the Bible; Genesis, Exodus, Leviticus, Numbers and Deuteronomy. These contain a cosmology and an historical account of the early years of the Jewish people. They also contain commandments and teachings covering every aspect of human existence, relationships with God, with fellow human beings and with the earth. However, in Jewish usage, Torah also has a much wider definition. Running parallel with the five books of Moses, sometimes also known as the written Torah, is a whole range of teachings and interpretations which expound the Torah. These are sometimes known as the oral Torah because they were originally passed on orally from one teacher to another, although they have been transmitted in written form for almost 2000 years.

The Jewish Bible also includes prophetical books, known as Nevi'im and the Writings, known as Ketuvim. The name most commonly given by Jews to the Bible is an acronym derived from these three divisions – TaNaKh (Torah, Nevi'im, Ketuvim).

Torah	Nevi'im	Ketuvim
Genesis	Joshua	Psalms
Exodus	Judges	Proverbs
Leviticus	Samuel I & II	Job
Numbers	Kings I & II	Song of Songs
Deuteronomy	Isaiah	Ruth
	Jeremiah	Lamentations
	Ezekiel	Ecclesiastes
	Hosea	Esther
	Joel	Daniel
	Amos	Ezra
	Obadiah	Nehemiah
	Jonah	Chronicles I & II
	Micah	
	Nahum	
	Habakkuk	
	Zephaniah	
	Haggai	
	Zechariah	
	Malachi	

The main elements of oral Torah are the Mishnah, codified around 200 C.E. and the Gemara which reached its final form around 500 C.E. The Mishnah (literally: repetition, teaching) is a thematic code of religious law and is divided into six sections:

Zera'im (seeds), dealing with prayer and agriculture

JEWISH BELIEFS ABOUT *TORAH*

From the *Torah*

Surely, this Instruction which I enjoin upon you this day is not too baffling for you, nor is it beyond reach. It is not in the heavens, that you should say 'Who among us can go up to the heavens and impart it to us that we may observe it?' Neither is it beyond the sea, that you should say 'Who among us can cross to the other side of the sea and get it for us and impart it to us, that we may observe it?' No, the thing is very close to you, in your mouth and in your heart, to observe it.

(Deuteronomy 30: 11–14)

From the Writings

Oh how I love your Torah! *It is my meditation all the day.*

(Psalm 119: 97)

From rabbinic literature

Study it (Torah) over and over again, for everything is contained in it. Contemplate it, spend your whole life with it, do not move away from it, for you can have no better guide than this.

(Sayings of the Fathers, 5: 25)

From the liturgy

With a deep love you have loved us, O Lord our God, with great and overflowing pity you have pitied us. Our Father, our King, for the sake of our fathers who trusted in you and to whom you taught the statutes of life, be gracious also to us and teach us. Our Father, merciful and compassionate Father, have mercy on us and put it into our hearts to understand and to discern, to hear, learn and teach, to heed, to do and to fulfill in love all the words of instruction in your Torah.

(from the morning prayers)

Mo'ed (fixed time) dealing with festivals

Nashim (women) dealing with marriage and divorce

Nezikin (torts), dealing with civil law, justice and ethics

Ķodoshim (holy things), dealing with food laws and offerings

Tohorot (purities), dealing with ritual purity.

The *Gemara* (literally, completion) takes the form of rabbinical debate and discussion on the *Mishnah* and the two works are incorporated together in the *Talmud*. There are two versions of the *Gemara*, one produced in the schools of Babylon and one by the schools in the land of Israel. Each contains written versions of the debates in the rabbinical academies of the two countries. Because it is more comprehensive and because the Babylonian school became the major centre for Jewish learning until around 1000 C.E., the Babylonian *Talmud* is generally regarded as more authoritative. It is also much more frequently studied.

Other elements of oral *Torah* have emerged through the centuries as commentaries have been written, codes have been compiled and responses to particular issues have been made. All of this vast body of traditional interpretation helps to form the Jew's understanding of *Torah*.

Authority

The status of the various elements of *Torah*, both written and oral, is one of the key areas for understanding the different groupings in Judaism. For Orthodox Jews, the written *Torah* is the revealed word of God and the oral *Torah* is its authoritative interpretation which was also re-vealed by God to Moses and handed on by Moses to his successors. They will therefore follow rabbinic guidance in determining matters of Jewish faith or practice, whether by consulting a work of rabbinic literature or by asking a question of the local rabbi. Throughout Jewish history, there have been different understandings of the issue. The oral *Torah* as we now have it is the development of Pharisaic Judaism (*circa* 150 B.C.E.). Other groups contemporary with the Pharisees, such as the Sadducees, rejected their under-standing of the oral *Torah*. In later periods, when the rabbinic approach had become normative, the Ķaraites (a group which originated in the eighth century – a very small number still follow their teachings) rejected the oral *Torah* and lived according to a very literal interpretation of the written *Torah*. Still later, the Reform and Liberal

Jews have tended to see the written *Torah* as divinely inspired but coloured by the history and social background of the several different authors whom God inspired; what it has to teach is therefore not necessarily eternally relevant or universally applicable. The oral *Torah*, in this view, is equally a product of a particular historical period and is not regarded as authoritative, although it may well be considered. The interpretations and conscience of the individual play a much greater role in determining Jewish practice for the Reform Jew.

God's instruction

The text of *Torah*, whether in its limited sense or its extended sense, is only the starting point. *Torah* is also a process, an endeavour to understand from the words of *Torah* what it is that God wants to teach his people, what it is that God wants them to do. To engage in study of *Torah* is to participate in revelation; *Torah* stems from God but human beings are its agents. If they do not study it, learn it and practise it, the 'circuit' of revelation is broken. Virtually all Jewish literature and a large part of the spiritual endeavour of the Jewish people through the ages can be seen as part of this process.

Practices surrounding the *Torah*

When teaching about the place of *Torah* in Judaism, it may be useful to look at examples of practices which reflect some of the beliefs and attitudes described above.

- Regular study of the *Torah*
- Regular reading of the *Torah* and from other parts of *Tanakh* as part of the synagogue service – use of biblical passages in liturgy
- Placing the scrolls of *Torah* in the ark at the far end of the synagogue and adorning them with richly decorated mantles and silver ornaments
- Processing the scrolls around the synagogue before and after the reading
- Kissing the scroll with a fringe of the *tallit* (prayer shawl) during the procession and before reading a passage from it
- Worshippers standing whenever the scroll is being carried and for the reading of certain passages
- Elevating the scroll for everyone to see before (the usual Sefardi custom) or after (the Ashkenazi custom) the reading
- The festival of *Simḥat Torah* (Rejoicing of the *Torah*).

Relationship to shared human experience

The centrality of *Torah* in Judaism obviously relates to the common human desire for an authoritative basis on which to pattern one's life and for guidelines by which values and beliefs can be measured. Many people wish to appeal to some authoritative source against which they can check, evaluate or confirm prevailing values and behaviour patterns. To be credible, such a source must have stood the test of time. It must reflect a knowledge or understanding which transcends their own limited understanding and values. It must embody an idealistic vision of what ought to be and what might be. It must present a realistic challenge to the quality of both personal and social life. For Jews, the *Torah* contains this kind of material. What distinguishes Jews is the way they use *Torah* in order to confirm or challenge their own and society's values and lifestyle. The way in which this actually takes place is further examined in the sections on *mitzvah* (below) and on the spirituality of the *Halakhah* (p. 25).

Mitzvah or commandment

Introduction

In Judaism, as we have already seen in the sections on *Torah* and belief in God, the necessary concomitant of revelation is action on the basis of that revelation. Humanity's task is to live a life of holiness according to God's commandments. The Hebrew word for commandment is *mitzvah* (plural: *mitzvot*) and the word is used to denote the individual units of God's instructions, the practical observances of *Torah*.

The tradition, reflected in the passage from the *Talmud* quoted on p. 14, that there are 613 *mitzvot*, is a very old one. In fact, there are far more than that and the number 613 is arrived at by *Gematria*, the exegetical tradition which bases its lessons on the numerical value of the Hebrew words. Hebrew has no separate symbols for numbers and uses the letters of the alphabet instead, so that A equals 1, B equals 2 and so on. Every Hebrew word can therefore be expressed as a number. The whole Jewish people is supposed to have heard the first two of the Ten Commandments and then to have been overwhelmed by the awesomeness of the moment of revelation, so that only Moses heard the rest of revelation directly from God, and then

transmitted it to the rest of the people. We are told that Moses 'commanded us *Torah*, the heritage of the community of Jacob' (Deuteronomy 33: 4). The numerical value of the letters that make up the Hebrew word *Torah* is 611, and the remaining two are the commandments heard by the whole people. The count of 613 is, however, generally accepted, although there have been several different attempts to classify and count them.

Positive and negative

The *mitzvot* can be classified according to their form – whether they are stated positively (you shall . . .) or negatively (you shall not . . .). In Rabbi Simlai's exegesis, the number 613 is divided into 365 negative commands, to correspond to the days of the year, and 248 positive commands, to correspond to the parts of the human body. In other words, the commandments embrace every moment of our existence and every part of our lives. Apart from the exegetical aspects, this sort of classification creates categories of commandments with some halakhic implications (implications for practical Jewish law). For instance, it is used to decide the religious obligations of women. Women, because of their commitments in the home, do not have to carry out positive commandments for which 'time is an essential factor', such as certain parts of the prayer service.

Mitzvot between human beings and between human beings and God

Another form of classification is to distinguish between commandments that govern inter-personal relations and those that govern relations between human beings and God. Examples of the former would be the commandments of feeding the hungry, not stealing, dealing honestly in business, and examples of the latter would be the duty to pray, to observe the Sabbath, and not to blaspheme God.

Obviously, the way in which we behave towards each other has profound implications for our relationship with God, a fact that is reflected by the constant references to the relationship between God and the Jewish people in those passages of the *Torah* which deal with the commandments about caring for other people. Breaking these commandments is seen as being as great a, if not a greater, *hillul haShem* (desecration of God), as breaking the *mitzvot* between God and humanity. The distinction is, however, important for the process of *teshuvah* (repentance), because the Day

From rabbinic writings

> *Rabbi Simlai said: 613 commandments were given to Moses, 365 negative commandments, corresponding to the days of the year, and 248 positive commandments, corresponding to the numbers of the parts of the body. Then David came and reduced them to 11 (cf. Psalm 15). Then came Isaiah and reduced them to six (cf. Isaiah 33: 15). Then came Micah and reduced them to 3 (cf. Micah 6: 8). Then Isaiah came again and reduced them to two, as it is said 'Keep judgement and do righteousness.' Then came Amos and reduced them to one, as it is said, 'Seek me and live.' Or one may say, then came Habakkuk and reduced them to one, as it is said, 'The righteous shall live by his faith.'*

> (Babylonian *Talmud*, Makkot 23b–24a)

of Atonement, a major observance in the Jewish calendar, is said to atone only for sins between humanity and God. For sins between people, remorse and the intention not to repeat the injury is not sufficient; an attempt must first be made to appease or make some restitution to the injured party.

Ḥukkim (statutes) and mishpatim (judgements)

A further distinction between different sorts of commandments is made on the basis of human understanding. For Orthodox Jews all the mitzvot are of divine origin, and are therefore to be followed to the best of their ability. The reasons for some of the commandments are, however, apparent. For instance, it is easy to see the reasons why one should not murder, why one should take care of widows and orphans. These commandments were classified as mishpatim or judgements. The reasons for the other category of commandments, God's statutes (ḥukkim) are not apparent to human understanding and commandments such as the dietary laws are obeyed simply because they are divine commands.

The idea of rationality became particularly important for mediæval Jewish philosophy, the greatest exponent of which was Maimonides, or Rabbi Moses ben Maimon, who lived in Spain from 1135 to 1204 and codified the law in Mishneh Torah (1180). The question whether it is possible or even desirable to seek the reasons for the commandments was much discussed. For some, God does not give commandments simply to test human obedience: there are reasons for every commandment, for instance the health benefits of keeping the dietary laws, and it is a perfectly proper religious endeavour to attempt to fathom those reasons. Maimonides was particularly concerned in his emphasis on the rational to be able to present Judaism as a wise and reasonable religion. For others, humanity's understanding is so far from the divine that the reasons for any of the commandments cannot be truly appreciated. The attempt can even lead to error if the person loses sight of the divine imperative behind the 'reason' perceptible to humanity.

Relationship to shared human experience

The framework of the mitzvot is the means by which the Jewish people is able to transfer the revelation of Torah into a practical and enactable way of life. It is perhaps this idea of numerous commandments which is most difficult for non-Jews to understand. It seems to militate against spirituality, against spontaneous religious expression and freedom of will.

In Judaism, the mitzvot are seen as a guide or as an expression of God's love for us and their observance as our side of the covenant. They embrace all of life and guide our every action. To have the mitzvot is seen as a great privilege and some practices reflect this – for instance the idea of Hiddur Mitzvah, beautification of the mitzvah. The mere carrying out of a mitzvah is often seen as an insufficient expression of the deep spiritual delight that it can bring, so the mitzvah is done in the most beautiful way possible. Instead of using any old cup for Ḳiddush, the prayer of sanctification on the Sabbath, a beautiful cup is used; the Torah scroll is decorated with silver ornaments, the poor invited into our homes are given the best food rather than left-overs.

The adherence to mitzvot raises a whole range of questions about human freedom and happiness, as well as the deeply felt need for order and pattern in life. The Jewish response is that the greatest happiness and the true experience of human freedom are to be found in a life of obedience, not of licence, and in a life of joyful dedication to God, not of selfish indulgence.

'Am Yisra'el or the people of Israel

Introduction

The origins of the Jewish people lie almost 4000 years ago, in the family of Abraham, the first of the patriarchs and founder of the Hebrew people (Genesis 11: 25). Jews regard Abraham as the first person to worship the one God. The family has become a very expanded and extended family but has nevertheless maintained its identity for all those years. Jewish identity is composed of many different elements and while for some, all the elements are an integral part of their make-up, for others, only one or two elements are enough to make them feel part of the Jewish people.

One of the most obvious elements in Jewish identity is biological. People are Jewish if they were born of a Jewish mother, by the Orthodox definition. Reform and Liberal Jews also accept someone as being of Jewish birth if only the father was Jewish, so long as the person concerned has had a Jewish upbringing. But this 'biological'

JEWISH BELIEFS ABOUT THE PEOPLE OF ISRAEL

From *Torah*

> *For you are a people consecrated to the Lord your God: of all the peoples on earth the Lord chose you to be his treasured people. It is not because you are the most numerous of peoples that the Lord set his heart on you and chose you – indeed, you are the smallest of peoples; but it was because the Lord favoured you and kept the oath he made to your fathers that the Lord freed you with a mighty hand and rescued you from the house of bondage, from the power of Pharaoh king of Egypt.*
>
> (Deuteronomy 7: 6–8)

From the Prophets

> *You are great indeed, O Lord God! There is none like you and there is no other God but you, as we have always heard. And who is like your people Israel, a unique nation on earth, whom God went and redeemed as his people, winning renown for himself and doing great and marvellous deeds for them and for your land – driving out nations and their gods before your people, whom you redeemed for yourself from Egypt. You have established your people Israel as your very own people for ever; and you, O Lord, have become their God.*
>
> (II Samuel 7: 22–24)

identity is only one way of being Jewish. A convert, who goes through the appropriate learning process and the conversion ceremony, is considered to be as much a child of Abraham as someone born a Jew, sharing fully in the inheritance of the Jewish people. Judaism is therefore more than a race, because Jewish identity has never been exclusively the property of one racial group.

The Jewish religion is another obvious part of the pattern. For converts, the only path of entry into the Jewish people is religious. It is religion that distinguished the Jews from their neighbours throughout history. For many Jews, their religion and the way of life which that implies is the most important part of their identity. For others, however, religion is not important and may even be obstructive; yet they still feel themselves to be part of the Jewish people. The phenomenon of the secular Jew is perhaps a surprising one to those of other religious traditions who consider their faith to be the most important factor in their identification with the group. The secular Jew may be an atheist or an agnostic; religious Jews will regard such a person as a full, though not an observant, member of the Jewish community. The case of a Jew who identifies with another religious community is more problematic; groups such as the Hebrew Christians are a case in point. Such groups claim that they can maintain their Jewish identity while professing another religion; most Jews, however, would regard positive self-identification with a different religious community as incompatible with Judaism.

A further element, and one that has been of increased importance in recent years, is national identity. From the return from slavery in Egypt in about 1290 B.C.E. to the land of Canaan until the destruction of the two Temples (in about 581 B.C.E. by the Babylonians, and in 70 C.E. by the Romans), the Jews had all the characteristics of a nation: a specific geographical area where they lived, national sovereignty, a common language, a common national history and purpose and a common religion. During the centuries of the Diaspora (the dispersal of the Jews among other nations) only the last three have applied, yet the national identity has remained. Since the re-establishment of the state of Israel in 1948, the first two have applied to those Jews who live in Israel. In this, as in other areas that go to make up Jewish identity, there is a very wide variety of responses. Some Jews find their national identity in Israel sufficient, and many secular Israeli Jews respond in this way. For some, living in Israel is a vital expression of their religious commitment. For others, Zionism is not a part of their religious identification and they maintain their identification in other countries of the world. Yet others might have no religious identity, nor do they feel the need to express their national identity by living in Israel, although they may support Israel in other ways.

The Chosen People

The cohesive nature of the Jewish people, despite the cultural diversity and dispersion of the Jews, has sometimes been the cause of misunderstanding and misinterpretation. It is worth examining in the context of R.E. some of the phrases such as 'the Chosen People', 'a kingdom of priests and a holy nation', 'a light to the nations', which express a particular facet of what Jews believe to be the spiritual function of their people but which have often been understood as indicating exclusivity and even arrogance.

In the Jewish world view, the Jews were chosen by God to fulfill a particular function. Such a choice does not imply that the Jews were the only people ever to have had a special relationship with God, but simply that for this specific task, the Jews were chosen as the vehicle. The function is receiving the *Torah,* God's instruction. The *Torah* was given to the Jews for the whole world. It is certainly seen as a privilege to have been chosen for such a task, but the responsibilities that the task entails are more significant. The mission of the Jewish people is to bring the whole world to an acknowledgement of God and to a recognition of the basic values and ethics that are implied by a belief in God. As such, Judaism is a universalistic and a missionary religion. It is, however, also a particularistic religion in that there is a certain pattern of life demanded of Jews as a part of their response to God. Non-Jews, as we have seen in the section on *Brit,* are not obliged to follow this particular path in order to follow God's teaching. The ultimate goal of the Jews is expressed in the *'Alenu* prayer, which concludes each of the three daily prayer services: 'We therefore hope in you, O Lord our God, that we may soon see the glory of your strength . . . when the world will be perfected under your almighty rule and all humanity will call on your name . . . let all of them accept the yoke of your kingdom so that you may rule over them soon and for ever. For the kingdom is yours and you will reign in glory for all eternity; the Lord shall be king over the whole earth and on that day the Lord will be One and known as One.'

Relationship to shared human experience

The strong feeling of belonging to a people that all Jews share is obviously a powerful response to the common human need for fellowship and a sense of identity. It provides bonds that extend far beyond immediate links with family and local community to include all Jews.

Free will and human nature

Introduction

Human beings have been created in the image of God: that is, in the image of one who, in the words of Jeremiah, acts with kindness, justice and equity in the world. The task of humanity is to be true to this divinely ordained character, to be God's partner in creating justice and righteousness in this world. There are two very important concepts in Judaism that relate to these ideas on human nature, the concept of the good and evil inclination and the concept of free will, which we shall explore in turn.

Yetzer haTov v 'Yetzer haRa

Judaism does not believe that human beings are inherently sinful. 'Adam, the first human being ('adam is the Hebrew term for 'human being', not primarily a masculine proper name) was the first person to sin but this sin had no spiritual effect on any other human being. Rather, it shows that all people have within them the capacity for good as well as the capacity for evil. The idea of the good and the evil inclination, the yetzer haTov and the yetzer haRa expresses this. These are internal (although in rabbinic literature they are sometimes personified) human impulses to righteous or evil actions. They are in essence equally balanced, even though, as the rabbis observed, 'one good deed leads to another and one sin leads to another' (Pirkei Avot 4: 2). All people, therefore, are fully responsible for their own actions, and are free to follow whichever inclination they choose.

There are also many rabbinic statements which extend the responsibility of the individual to the whole world, expressing the idea that the balance of good and evil in the world is equal. All people should therefore regard their good deeds as pushing the world's balance toward the side of good, and their evil deeds as pushing the balance

over to the side of evil. Obviously, the *Torah* has an important role to play in this connection, providing guidance, inspiration and assistance for humanity in its attempt to live up to its divine nature.

The nature of evil itself is seen in a particular way in Judaism. As Isaiah says, God creates both good and evil (Isaiah 45: 7). Perhaps as a reaction against Zoroastrian and Gnostic theology, Judaism has resisted very strongly the idea of an evil force or devil, independent of and opposed to God. The biblical Satan is one of the angels whose job it is to be the accuser or the adversary, the prosecuting counsel, so to speak, who takes note of all of humanity's wrong deeds. He is allowed, in the story of Job, to inflict suffering on Job to see how he will react, but he does not actually tempt Job to do wrong. He is also subject to God, rather than a devil opposing God.

Free will

Two of the classic paradoxes of theistic faith are that God is all-powerful yet humanity is free to act as it chooses, and that God is all-knowing yet humanity's actions are not determined. It is in the context of free will, freedom to choose good or evil, that Jewish ideas about the eventual judgement of the soul are developed. Everyone has the capacity to become, as Maimonides says, 'as righteous as Moses or as wicked as Jeroboam'; furthermore, everyone, however wicked, has the possibility and capacity for repentance.

Life and death

Life is seen as one of God's supreme gifts and is valued very highly. As the psalm says, 'the dead cannot praise God, nor any who go down into silence – but we will bless the Lord now and forever' (Psalm 115: 18). The preservation of life is an important duty and takes priority over all but three of the commandments of *Torah* (the exceptions being idolatry, murder and adultery). The *Torah* itself is described as 'a Tree of Life' and as its commandments can only be fulfilled in this world, to act upon it is humanity's highest task.

Despite this emphasis on the importance and value of life, there is a strong belief in Judaism in an after-life and the immortality of the soul. A prayer read each morning expresses this: 'My God, the soul which you have placed within me is pure. You have created it, you have formed it, you have breathed it into me. You preserve it within me; you will take it from me and restore it to me in the

JEWISH BELIEFS ABOUT HUMAN NATURE

From *Torah*

God said 'let us make man in our image, after our likeness. They shall rule the fish of the sea, the birds of the sky, the cattle, the whole earth, and all the creeping things that creep on the earth.' God created man in his image, in the image of God he created them; male and female he created them.

(Genesis 1: 26–27)

You shall be holy, for I, the Lord your God, am holy.

(Leviticus 19: 2)

From the Writings

When I behold your heavens, the work of your fingers, the moon and stars that you set in place, what is man that you have been mindful of him, that you have made him little less than divine, and adorned him with glory and majesty; you have made him master over your handiwork . . .

(Psalm 8: 4–7)

From rabbinic writings

A single man was first created in the world, to teach that if any man causes a single soul to perish, it is as though he has caused an entire world to perish, and if any man saves a single soul, it is as though he had saved an entire world.

(*Mishnah*, Sanhedrin 4: 5)

Everything is foreseen by God, yet free will is granted to man.

(*Mishnah*, Avot 3: 19)

Man has been given free will: if he wishes to turn toward the good way and to be righteous, the power is in his own hands; if he wishes to turn toward the evil way and to be wicked, the power is likewise in his own hands. Thus it is written in the Torah: 'And the Lord God said, Behold, the man is become as one of us, to know good and evil.' This means that in regard to this matter, the species of man became single of its kind in this world and that no other species is like it. Man knows good and evil out of himself, out of his intelligence and reason.

(Moses Maimonides)

hereafter.' Because the soul is immortal and because there will eventually be a judgement of some kind, human actions in this world have profound importance and implications for the life of the world to come.

Relationship to shared human experience

Jewish beliefs about human nature and the significance of human action reflect the common search for meaning, purpose and value in human existence. This search for meaning relates to all those questions about what makes human beings human, and about the relationship between human beings and other creatures and the earth we all share. Most religions or belief systems will attempt in some way or another to respond to such questions.

Judaism sets out to provide a framework of belief in which these questions may be approached. It also gives moral teachings and sustains a range of values which, for Jews, help them act in a way consistent with their beliefs about the task of humanity.

Humanity's position in the world view of Judaism is very high. This position does not carry with it superiority, however, but responsibility. Humanity is responsible for its actions in the moral sphere, it is responsible for other forms of life on this planet and it is responsible for its stewardship of the earth. The Hebrew word for humanity, *adam,* is closely linked with the word for earth, *adamah,* and the interdependence of human beings and the earth is emphasised in Jewish tradition through commandments showing concern for the land, its produce and the creatures that live on it. In these ways, Judaism provides channels through which the humanity of Jews can be expressed as part and parcel of the religious framework.

Teshuvah or repentance

Introduction

Jewish ideas about repentance are closely connected with ideas on the nature of humanity and sin. As we have seen in the section on free will and the nature of humanity, people are not seen as being inherently sinful. Each person comes into the world in a state of equilibrium, neither good nor evil. Each act committed by that person swings the balance to one side or the other, depending on the nature of the act. Ideally, each person should

do good, rather than evil, and the words of *Torah* are there to provide inspiration and guidance. However, people do not always do the right thing, and the state of equilibrium is disturbed. The root meaning of one of the Hebrew words for sin is 'to miss' and this perhaps also indicates something of the Jewish view on the nature of sin and repentance. The process by which equilibrium is restored is called in Hebrew *teshuvah,* which literally means returning.

The process of *teshuvah*

Teshuvah is something that can, and should, take place at any time. The first stage of the process comes with the recognition that a sin of some sort has been committed, and with feelings of regret and a desire to repent.

The next stage depends on the nature of the transgression. If the act involved one of the *mitzvot* between humanity and God, the desire to repent and the resolve never to do the same thing again is sufficient. If, however, it involved one of the interpersonal *mitzvot,* there must first be an act of reconciliation. This means that the offender must seek out the person who has been hurt and ask his or her forgiveness. Although *teshuvah,* as we have said, may take place at any time, it comes to the forefront during the Ten Days of Repentance before *Yom Kippur.* At this time many people will ask forgiveness of family and friends for any things they might have done to hurt them during the year that has passed.

Once forgiveness has been obtained or recompense made, the offender asks for God's forgiveness – many of the texts on *teshuvah* emphasise God's abundant mercy and the fact that the gates of repentance are always open. The final stage, and true test, of *teshuvah* comes when the opportunity to commit the same act occurs and the person does not sin again.

In Judaism, the emphasis is always on the capacity and the duty of each person to review their actions continually. Everyone has free will and the possibility of returning in repentance is open to all. The entire process of repentance, from recognition of wrong-doing to God's forgiveness, is within the power of each person.

The *Ba'al Teshuvah*

Just as Judaism believes that no one is inherently sinful, it also believes that no one is irredeemably sinful. However many sins someone has committed, the possibility of repentance is always

JEWISH BELIEFS ABOUT REPENTANCE

From *Torah*

When all these things befall you – the blessing and the curse that I have set before you – and you take them to heart amidst the various nations to which the Lord your God has banished you, and you return to the Lord your God, and you and your children heed his command with all your heart and soul, just as I enjoin upon you this day, then the Lord your God will restore your fortunes and take you back in love.

(Deuteronomy 30: 1–3)

From rabbinic writings

Who is a true penitent? Rabbi Judah said: The man who, when the same opportunity for sin occurs once more, refrains from sinning.

(Babylonian *Talmud*, Yoma 86b)

A king had a son who had gone astray from his father a journey of a hundred days; his friends said to him 'Return to your father.' He said, 'I cannot.' Then his father sent to say, 'Return as far as you can, and I will come to you the rest of the way.' So God says, 'Return to me, and I will return to you.'

(Pesiḳta Rabati, 184b)

'Teach us to number our days' (Psalm 90: 12). Rabbi Joshua said: If we knew exactly the number of our days, we should repent before we die. Rabbi Eliezer said: Repent one day before you die. His disciples said 'Who knows when he will die?' All the more, then, let him repent today, for perhaps he will die tomorrow. The result is that all his life will be spent in repentance.

(*Midrash* Psalms on Psalm 90: 12)

available. A person who completely reforms their way of life and returns to Judaism is known as a *Ba'al Teshuvah,* literally a master of returning. There have been *Ba'alei Teshuvah* throughout the history of Judaism but the term is used nowadays to refer to the significant number of Jews from non-traditional or areligious backgrounds who have returned to greater levels of belief and practice. There are now *yeshivot,* centres of Jewish learning, in Israel, New York and some other cities, which cater specifically for people who come with little or no knowledge of traditional Jewish learning.

Relationship to shared human experience

Any system which aims to provide a framework for living must reckon with the possibility that its guidelines will not always be adhered to. If the guidelines are vested with any kind of authority, those who stray from them will have to come to terms with feelings of remorse and a desire to return to the correct path. There must therefore be some mechanism which enables them to come to terms with and work through such feelings. The process of *teshuvah* provides such a mechanism for the system of Judaism.

The process of *teshuvah* also provides a very clear framework for the various stages of repentance. If *teshuvah* is to have a real effect on a person's actions and personality, they must be able to come to terms with each stage of the process and understand the meaning it has for their lives, before moving on to the next stage.

Messiah and redemption

Introduction

Belief in a redemption, the establishment of God's kingdom and the inauguration of an era of peace and knowledge of God have always been features of Judaism and one of its main messages of hope. As with most ideas in Judaism, the messianic idea has developed throughout history and takes several different forms. It has also developed as a response to history: the roots of the idea are found in the promises made by God to David and to Solomon. After the division of the kingdom and particularly after the destruction of the First Temple, the prophetic ideas about the kingdom of God and a time when 'nation shall not take up sword against nation, they shall never again know war' (Isaiah 2: 4) are found. Mishnaic ideas about

the Messiah must be seen against the background of the Roman occupation of Palestine and the rabbis' hopes for the ending of Roman rule and the exile of the Jewish people.

The main elements of the messianic idea are that a descendant of the House of David will be appointed by God to inaugurate an age of peace, when Israel will be gathered from all corners of the world and when all of humanity will know that there is only one God. The term 'Messiah' is derived fromt he Hebrew *Mashiah* which means 'anointed'. In its original Biblical usage, it is applied to any king – part of the coronation ritual was anointing – and then came to be applied in general to kings or prophets who were entrusted by God with a particular function (cf. Isaiah 45: 1, 61: 1). It was later used exclusively to refer to this descendant of David.

Natural and supernatural

Different aspects of the messianic idea have been emphasised by various Jewish thinkers and the two main trends of thought can be characterised as naturalistic and supernatural.

The supernatural view would see the pattern of history as pre-determined. The Messiah will come at a time that is already fixed. There might well be a period of catastrophic events before the messianic kingdom is established and that kingdom will be utopian. This view would also stress the idea of a personal Messiah and the miraculous nature of his gifts, although Judaism has always strongly rejected the idea that the Messiah is in any way divine.

The naturalistic view envisages a future that evolves from the present and is not radically different, except for universal peace and knowledge of God. It is to be brought about by human effort and obedience to God's will, not by cataclysmic events. This view might also be more likely to stress the idea of a messianic age, or the Messiah in each human being, rather than a single charismatic leader who is the Messiah. The universalistic aspects of Jewish messianism will also be emphasised.

Christian and Jewish messianism

It is particularly important for teachers when looking at this aspect of Jewish belief to be aware of the distinctions between Jewish and Christian messianism. Christian messianism uses much of the same language as Jewish messianism but gives very different significance to some of the terms.

JEWISH BELIEFS ABOUT THE MESSIAH

From the Prophets

In the days to come, the Mount of the Lord's house shall stand firm among the mountains and tower above the hills; and all the nations shall gaze on it with joy. And the many peoples shall go and say: 'Come, let us go up to the Mount of the Lord to the house of the God of Jacob; that he may instruct us in his ways and that we may walk in his paths.' For instruction shall come forth from Zion, the word of God from Jerusalem. Thus he will judge among the nations and arbitrate for the many peoples, and they shall beat their swords into ploughshares and their spears into pruning hooks: nation shall not take up sword against nation; they shall never again know war.

(Isaiah 2: 2–4)

Thus said the Lord God, 'I am going to take the Israelite people from among the nations they have gone to and gather them from every quarter and bring them to their own land . . . then they shall be my people and I will be their God. My servant David shall be king over them; there shall be one shepherd for all of them. They shall follow my rules and faithfully obey my laws. Thus they shall remain in the land which I gave to my servant Jacob and in which your fathers dwelt; they and their children and their children's children shall dwell there forever, with my servant David as their prince for all time. I will make a covenant of friendship with them – it shall be an everlasting covenant with them . . .

(Ezekiel 37: 21, 23–26)

From rabbinic writings

Rabbi Joshua ben Levi met Elijah . . . he asked him, 'When will the Messiah come?' Elijah replied, 'Go and ask him.' 'But where is he ?' 'At the gate of Rome.' Rabbi Joshua went and said to him, 'Peace be with you, master and rabbi.' He replied 'Peace be with you, son of Levi.' He said, 'When is the master coming?' He replied, 'Today.' Then Rabbi Joshua returned to Elijah . . . and said, 'He spoke falsely to me, for he said he would come today, and he has not come.' Then Elijah said, 'He meant "Today, if you would but hearken to his voice" (Psalm 95: 7)'.

(Babylonian *Talmud*, Sanhedrin 98a)

From the liturgy

May all the inhabitants of the world realise and know that to you every knee must bend, every tongue must vow allegiance. May they bend the knee and prostrate themselves before you, Lord our God, and give honour to your glorious name; may they all accept the yoke of your kingdom, so that you may reign over them soon, forever and ever. For the kingdom is yours and to all eternity you will reign in glory, as it is written in your Torah, 'The Lord shall be king forever and ever.' And it is said 'The Lord shall be king over all the earth; on that day, the Lord shall be One and his name One.'

(the *'Alenu* prayer)

We will therefore indicate some of the major variations.

The most important difference, from the Jewish point of view, is the status of the Messiah. The Messiah may have some miraculous powers, may have charismatic qualities as a leader, may have been appointed to this task by God. The Messiah is, however, always represented as a human being and not God, who alone is the Redeemer. The Christian idea of the Messiah as a cosmic agent of redemption and as God incarnate is blasphemous to the Jew.

The other area of concern is the question of what the Messiah is to achieve. Jewish messianism stresses the goal of real peace and would expect the Messiah, or the messianic age, to bring this about. Jews must therefore reject the claims of those who say they are the Messiah – and there have been many throughout Jewish history – but do not bring true peace to this world.

The idea of redemption itself is also very different in Judaism and Christianity. Judaism sees redemption as referring to the liberation of the Jews and ultimately of all humanity from persecution and oppression, so that, in the words of Maimonides, 'they will have no other occupation than to know the Lord'.

Obviously, these questions are of fundamental importance to both faiths, particularly in view of their shared heritage and close relationship. It is therefore vital for them to be presented in a way which is both true to each faith and sensitive to the areas of tension.

The role of Zionism

A constant element of all the traditional interpretations of Messianism has been the return to the land of Israel and the ingathering of the exiles from all the corners of the world. In the late 19th century, the modern Zionist movement grew up in parallel with many other nationalist movements of the time. It took many of its elements from traditional religious Zionism, while also promoting the establishment of an independent homeland for the Jewish people as a practical political goal. Many Jews saw Zionism as a secular version of traditional messianism and the return of the Jews to their own land as a fulfilment of all their hopes. This has led to one of the areas of conflict that now exist between secular and some religious Jews in Israel. The latter see the secular state of Israel as an insult to the Messiah, a pre-empting of messianic prerogatives and role, and a denial of God's plan for redemption. Other religious Jews, while acknowledging that the state of Israel has imperfections and is not the complete fulfilment of the messianic ideal, see its establishment as miraculous and as the beginning of redemption.

Relationship to shared human experience

Human beings have a capacity to reflect on the future as well as the present. This reflection often gives rise to visions, images and hopes of a better, fairer, more peaceful world to live in.

Jewish ideas about redemption and about the role of the Messiah who is to inaugurate the life of the world to come provide a message of hope and a sense of purpose for the life of this world.

The universalistic aspects of this area of Jewish belief reflect the strong concern in Judaism for humanity as a whole. The redemption is for all humanity; the cessation of war and the beginning of peace will benefit the whole world. Such beliefs obviously provide a response to common human fears in the face of the destructive forces of this world and the inevitability of death. Many of the beliefs outlined above developed in Judaism as a very direct response to the vicissitudes of the Jewish people as they have been subjected to persecution, suffering and oppression at different stages through history. They therefore appeal to many of the emotions such as fear, powerlessness, or a sense of purposelessness that are experienced by everybody. At the same time, they provide hope for the future. They enable the Jew to look forward to a time when the supreme values of Judaism, knowledge and love of God, will be unchallenged.

PART THREE

Jewish spirituality

Introduction

In the circle model used at the beginning of the manual (page 1) to indicate some aspects of this world religion, we have shown various beliefs and concepts which lie at the core of Judaism. We have already examined the beliefs, the abstract ideas on which the religion is based. We now turn to the area of spirituality, a more complex topic and one which is much less easily conveyed in a textbook. It is also much less easily conveyed in an explicit form in the context of R.E., except in the upper secondary years. However, it is vital even for teachers of younger age-groups to be aware of the importance of Jewish spirituality and to perceive the connections between it and Jewish practice.

The circle model shows clearly that beliefs, spirituality and practice are closely interrelated. In order to understand any aspect of Judaism, the relation to belief and spirituality must be taken into account. For example, a religious practice such as giving charity obviously depends on an acceptance of the core beliefs, particularly those about God and the nature and duties of humanity. It is also for the Jew a spiritual experience, a transferral of the written word of *Torah* into action in the world.

In any religion, an attempt to define and describe the nature of its spirituality will be a very difficult task. This is particularly so of Judaism, where spirituality certainly exists but rather than being explicitly stated, is implicit in the obligations and duties that the covenantal relationship imposes on Jews. Jewish spirituality is the spirituality of the *Halakhah*; attempting to carry out the word of God and perceive the will of God as it has been revealed in the *Torah*. It is the spirituality of Jewish prayer and the spirituality of the values that Judaism attempts to inculcate.

Spirituality of the *Halakhah*

The word *halakhah* derives from a Hebrew root which means to walk or to go. It is used to describe the system of Jewish law, so it implies that Jewish law is a way, a path. Eliezer Berkowitz in his book *Not in Heaven*[1] defines *Halakhah* as 'the bridge over which the *Torah* moves from the written word to the living deed'. The written word is set and fixed; the *Halakhah* is dynamic, reflecting the tension of the interaction between *Torah* and the ever-changing demands and problems of human life. The *Halakhah* also depends on human beings – the *Torah* is given by God but its being put into practice depends entirely on those who receive it. Their doing so provides them with a link with God and a vital source of spirituality in their lives.

The *Torah* is viewed by Orthodox Jews as direct revelation and by non-fundamentalist Jews as at least divinely inspired, so that those who set down the words of *Torah* are considered to have had some awareness of a transcendent source for what they wrote. All the commandments of *Torah* therefore, reflect the presence of God and show that there is nothing in human lives that cannot be seen in terms of *Torah*. This applies as much to commandments about what to do if something borrowed from a friend is lost or damaged while in your possession as to commandments about

[1] Published by Ktav, New York, 1983.

25

prayer or love of God. The force of this is to spiritualise all action and all of life.

This spiritualisation can only be achieved if the awareness of the transcendental nature of the *Halakhah* is maintained. Many of the *mitzvot*, the commandments, of the *Torah* benefit either the person who carries out the *mitzvah* or the person for whom it is done. If, however, this is the only motivation for performing the *mitzvah*, the act is no longer a spiritual one. It must be carried out as a response to transcendental demands that one should act in this way. It must also reflect a feeling that the action itself is of more than temporary significance: that its implementation fits into the divine plan for the universe and that the person who carries it out thereby does God's will and participates in God's revelation.

The idea of humanity's partnership with God in the world through implementation of the *Torah* is a bold one but one that is often found in rabbinic sources. It is an idea which is particularly emphasised by the mystic strand in Judaism. Many of the foremost mystics were deeply involved in the halakhic process – for instance Joseph Karo, the author of the *Shulḥan Arukh* (1564–5), the most influential code of *Halakhah* ever produced, was a Spanish Jewish mystic – a fact which is in itself an interesting reminder for those who see the defining of the minutiae of religious law as anything but spiritual. In the *Ḳabbalah*, the mystical tradition, the idea of *tiḳḳun olam* is expounded. This is based on the view that creation caused a disunity in the world, and divine sparks were scattered throughout the entire universe. Humanity's task is to work to reunite or repair the world – *tiḳḳun olam* literally means 'repairing the world'. The way in which the world can be repaired is, of course, by carrying out the *mitzvot* of the *Torah*, and each righteous action goes some way towards the cosmic task of reunification, a task that will eventually lead to redemption. The implications of this view are enormous, particularly in the emphasis they place on the significance of human action. *Torah* was given to humanity, it can only be carried out in this world and it is the means by which the world is to be redeemed. Several mystical works make this quite clear, going deeply into the spiritual meaning of each of the *mitzvot*, however 'unspiritual' they may seem on the surface.

The other aspect of human responsibility for the *Halakhah* is the responsibility to learn about it. As we have seen, the ultimate aim of *Torah* is that it should be put into practice. In order to do that, it must be studied so that what it has to teach becomes internalised. As we will see in the section on study, learning *Torah* is also a form of spiritual expression. Repeated study of the words of God is a way of coming closer to God, closer to an understanding of the values and stances that *Torah* communicates. Again, there are many passages from rabbinic sources which reflect this idea; the most famous is probably the story of the oven of Akhnai, found in the *Talmud*. In this story, the rabbis had debated the fitness for use of an oven. The rabbis disagreed, with one rabbi, Rabbi Eliezer, holding out against the majority of his colleagues. On the basis of a principle stated elsewhere in the *Talmud*, that the ruling should be according to majority opinion, Rabbi Eliezer should have backed down. Instead, he called on a series of divine miracles to prove that he was right. Despite the miracles, one of the majority stood up and said 'It is not in heaven' (Deuteronomy 30: 12) – in other words, emphasising that since the *Torah* has been given to humanity, it is a human responsiblity to interpret it, understand it and practise it here on earth, according to the principles of *Torah*. It is a process that must, by its nature, take place on the basis of human effort and understanding rather than on the basis of divine intervention. Because of this, study is always strongly emphasised in Judaism, for lay people as much as for the teachers who are the rabbis. By study, the individual is able to become God's partner, learning and implementing God's will in the world.

Jewish values

Despite the emphasis on study, there are elements of *Torah* which it can be difficult to absorb simply through reading. As will be seen in the section on study (p. 31), Jewish *Torah* study is intended to be interactive. The student should have a teacher and should study with others whenever possible. The 'Torah lifestyle' of someone who has internalised its teachings in itself communicates a great deal of *Torah*, particularly the values and stances which it inculcates. Most of these values reflect in some way Jewish ideas about the nature of God, in that humanity, through living the life of *Torah*, is supposed, as far as is possible, to take on some of the attributes of God.

Love

The most important of these values is undoubtedly love and love's corollary, compassion. God is repeatedly referred to as *HaRahaman*, the compassionate one, and God's love for humanity is emphasised in Torah as well as in liturgy. Equally, Israel's obligation to love God is one of the most important commandments, as we have seen in the *Shema*, the reading from Deuteronomy which forms part of the daily prayers:

> 'Hear O Israel! The Lord is our God, the Lord alone. You shall love the Lord your God with all your heart and with all your soul and with all your might.'

Just as the *Torah* has been given in love, so it is supposed to be fulfilled in love. The ideal of love extends also to all human beings, as expressed in the 'Golden Rule' of *Torah*, 'you shall love your fellow as yourself' (Leviticus 19: 18).

One may question whether 'love' is something that can be commanded. The rabbinic response is to remind us that actions can certainly be commanded. The Jew is obliged to act in a loving way to everyone and, as we shall see in the section on Jewish practices (p. 29), action in Judaism is generally regarded as leading to the state of mind implied by the action. In other words, where love does not yet exist, loving actions will cause love to grow. The section on personal life in Jewish practice details some of the ways in which this value is expressed in Jewish living.

Justice

Justice is another very important value and has many far-reaching implications for Jewish life. Much of *Halakhah* is devoted to the establishment of a just society and therefore to inculcating the ideal of justice. 'Justice' in this sense includes not only obvious elements, such as legal justice or just dealing in business but also just distribution of resources. The literal meaning of the Hebrew term used for 'charity', *tzedakah*, is justice. The implication of this is that to give charity is merely to act 'justly', to reapportion something of what one possesses and can manage without to those who stand in greater need of it.

Justice in the more obvious sense is also a high ideal in Judaism, so much so that it is one of the 'seven commandments of the sons of Noah', the basic commandments that all humanity, Jews and non-Jews alike are, in Jewish tradition, expected to observe. Living under a system of justice is seen as one of the things that distinguishes us from the generation of the flood (Genesis 9: 18 – 10: 32) who lived a life of wanton cruelty. It also illustrates something of the nature of *Halakhah*, that this area of Jewish spirituality expresses itself through the medium of practical and social action. The effectual sphere of Jewish spirituality is not so much the individual's own internal life as the individual's relation with society; the task is not building the kingdom of God within, but building it in the world.

Holiness

The Hebrew term for holiness, *kedusha*, derives from a root that means separate, distinct. God's holiness implies complete 'otherness', the qualities which make God so much greater than anything humanity can comprehend. In human terms, it implies actions or attitudes which elevate normal everyday concerns above their mundane nature and give them a flavour of the divine. The paradox of this aspect of Jewish spirituality is that such actions bring holiness into daily life and bring a direct awareness of the holy, the absolutely 'other' God.

Many of the commandments of *Torah* have this tendency, often explicitly stated. The most obvious example is the so-called 'Holiness Code', found in the 19th chapter of the book of Leviticus. The commandments found in this section deal with all sorts of areas of life: relations with other people, parents, neighbours, widows and orphans, and the poor; relations with God: observing the Sabbath, not worshipping idols, offering sacrifices; relations with the land and with animals. Holiness is therefore not simply a matter of a division between sacred and mundane. Indeed, in many cases, the commandments serve to take an action which might seem mundane and make it sacred, for instance the laws dealing with food. The eating of food is a basic, physical act, common to all living beings, human and animal alike. By following the requirements of the food laws, it is raised above the animal and becomes something holy, a form of religious expression.

The blessing recited before carrying out a commandment reflects this process. The blessing begins 'Blessed are you, Lord our God, King of the Universe, who has made us holy by your commandments and commanded us to . . .'. The intention of the blessing is to concentrate the mind of those carrying out the commandment and to remind them of the effect it should have on their life. Obviously, although the tendency of this concept is to emphasise the sacredness of all life, there are levels of holiness. Distinctions can be made, for instance the Sabbath is more holy than the other days of the week, the *Torah* is more holy than the prophetical books of the Bible and so on.

As we have stated above, the way in which all of these and other Jewish values are traditionally imparted is as much by direct example as by study of books. The existence of a class of rabbinic literature known as *musar*, or ethics, must not be ignored, nor its importance in Jewish teaching. Nevertheless, the use of living mentors or the study of the lives of people who embodied the ideals of *Torah* is extremely significant. It is also a course which should recommend itself to the teacher who wishes to convey something of this area of spirituality to younger pupils. They may not be able to deal with the abstract ideas that such lives presuppose but can absorb a great deal from the implicit message they contain. Rabbi Joseph Soloveitchik in a famous book called *Halakhic Man*[2] has expanded this idea. In this philosophical treatise on the nature of the *Halakhah* and the personality who is steeped in it, he posits the existence of 'halakhic man', who bridges the gap between the world of science and rationality and the world of religion. The quality of holiness and the quality of mind exuded by such a person is the essence of the spiritual nature of the *Halakhah*.

[2] *Published by the Jewish Publication Society, Philadelphia, 1983*

PART FOUR

Jewish practices

In the previous chapters, we have seen that the Jewish religion is based on a series of principles and beliefs. It also demands a whole range of practices and a particular lifestyle. The *Torah,* God's instruction to the Jewish people, has little value if it is not put into practice in daily life. The order of words in Exodus 24: 8, 'We will do and we will hear', is taken by the rabbis to indicate the vital importance of the actions and practice of Jews. However, the widely varying ways in which revelation and the status of *Torah* can be understood bring in their train different levels of practice and different interpretations of what it means to observe the *mitzvot.* Jews make their own responses to the commandments of God, so that gross generalisations are necessary in order to give an overall picture of Jewish practice. This fact should constantly be borne in mind while using this part of the book.

The mere performance of the *mitzvot* is only half the story. Two very important concepts save Judaism from becoming a religion of mechanical behaviourism and greatly add to the power of the *mitzvot.* They are *kavannah,* a Hebrew word which means direction or intention, and *liShmah,* the Hebrew for 'for its own sake'. *Kavannah* requires that when Jews carry out a particular *mitzvah,* they should do so with awareness of what they are doing and of the significance of their actions. This is one of the reasons why a blessing is recited before performing many of the *mitzvot,* in order to concentrate the mind on the action and its meaning. *LiShmah* requires that the *mitzvah* be carried out precisely because it is a *mitzvah,* a command of God, and not for any ulterior motive. An example of these two principles at work is in the *mitzvah* of prayer. When one prays, one should be intensely aware of the presence of God and

therefore aware of the direction of one's prayers (*kavannah*). To help people to achieve this, many synagogues have the verse 'Know before whom you stand' written above the ark. Jews should also be praying because they believe God wants them to do so and not in order to feel good about their own piety or in order to gain any particular benefit for themselves (*liShmah*). These two concepts should be borne in mind by teachers when helping pupils to explore the concrete practices of Judaism so that they gain an understanding not only of the observable externals but also of the underlying beliefs and spiritual experiences to which the *mitzvot* give expression.

Personal life

Introduction

Judaism lays great emphasis on the individual and the individual's response to the revelation of God. The rabbinic interpretation of Deuteronomy 29: 15 is that at the time of the revelation on Mount Sinai, not only the Jews alive at that time but also every Jewish soul ever in existence stood at the foot of the mountain to receive the *Torah* of God. This interpretation expresses the belief that each individual Jew is the direct recipient of revelation and is called to respond to it.

Obviously, individuals will respond to the traditions and practices of Judaism in a way that reflects their own needs, circumstances and level of belief. As a rule, people will then gravitate towards a Jewish community whose response is roughly similar to their own.

The *Torah* provides guidance for every aspect and activity of one's daily life but we will investigate three particular areas in order to begin to understand how Judaism forms and influences the individual's personal life.

Prayer

There are three main types of prayer recognised in Judaism: *tehilla*, praise of God; *hoda'ah*, thanksgiving; and *bakashah*, request. The basic unit of Jewish prayer is the *berakhah*, or blessing, which usually begins with the formula 'Blessed are you, Lord our God, King of the Universe'.

Judaism tries to maintain a balance between a fixed liturgy and spontaneity in prayer. Prayer, like any other form of communication, must be learned and will not necessarily happen at all if it is to depend only on spontaneous inspiration. The adult male Jew must therefore pray three times a day, in the morning, afternoon and evening (*Shaharit, Minhah* and *'Arvit/Ma'ariv*) and this sequence of prayers shapes the structure of the day for the traditional Jew. Women, because of their commitments in the home, have to pray only twice a day, in the morning and afternoon. The timing of the three daily prayers has a direct relationship with the times of sacrifices offered in the Jerusalem Temple before its destruction in 70 C.E.; the *'Avodah* (service) of the Temple has been replaced by the *'Avodat haLev* (service of the heart) that we offer with our prayers. Jewish prayers are almost always chanted, rather than said.

The two basic building blocks of all the services are the *Shema* and the *'Amidah*. The core of the *Shema* is a reading made up of three passages from *Torah*: Deuteronomy 6: 4–9; Deuteronomy 11: 13–21 and Numbers 15: 37–41. The first of these passages being 'Hear (*Shema*) O Israel, the Lord is our God, the Lord alone' and this forms the fundamental declaration of the faith of 'the people of Israel', a declaration which should be the last words spoken by Jews on their death beds. It has been used as part of the liturgy at least as far back as the time of the Second Temple. The *'Amidah* or Standing Prayer is also very ancient and some form of it probably also existed at the time of the Second Temple. It consists of 19 blessings, originally 18, hence the other name by which it is known, the *Shemoneh Esreh* or Eighteen, arranged in order of praise of the God of the Patriarchs; God, who will restore the dead to life, the holy God (blessings 1–3); petitions for knowledge, repentance, forgiveness, redemption, healing, a fruitful year, ingathering of the exiles, righteous judges, destruction of heretics and other enemies,

reward for the righteous, rebuilding of Jerusalem, the coming of the Messiah, and acceptance of prayer (blessings 4–16); and prayers for the return to Zion, thanksgiving for God's goodness and for the gift of peace (blessings 17–19). Finally there is a time for meditation and private prayer. The middle 13 blessings of petition are omitted on the Sabbath and festivals and are replaced by a special blessing for the Sabbath or festival day.

The morning service, *Shaharit*, is the longest, particularly on Mondays and Thursdays when the *Torah* is read as part of the service. The structure of the morning prayer is of introductory prayers and psalms so that the service starts with *tehilla*, the praise of God; the blessings preceding and following the recitation of the *Shema*; the *'Amidah* and concluding prayers. The afternoon prayer consists mainly of the *'Amidah*, preceded by a psalm and followed by a concluding prayer. The evening prayer consists of the *Shema* and its blessings, the *'Amidah* and concluding prayers.

At many other times during the day, there will be moments of prayer. There are blessings, known as the blessings of the senses (*birkhot hanehenin*) which refer to experiences of the five senses. They are said before eating any food, after food, on seeing beautiful or strange things in nature, on seeing a rainbow, on meeting a learned person, on smelling spices, on hearing thunder and on many other occasions. There is a tradition that one should say one hundred blessings every day and, including the blessings of the daily services, it is not at all difficult to find one hundred opportunities during the day to remember God and give witness to God's goodness. There are also blessings before carrying out particular *mitzvot* which help to create an atmosphere of *kavannah*.

Alongside this pattern of formalised prayer, which is found printed in the Jewish prayer book (*Siddur*), there exists a tradition of spontaneous communication with God. We have mentioned the time for private prayer at the conclusion of the *'Amidah*; there is also the practice of praying to God, often in the vernacular or the language in which the individual is most comfortable, known as *hitbodedut* or being alone with God. This practice is particularly emphasised by the Hasidim.

The fixed prayer services can be said anywhere. If possible, it is preferable to pray with the *minyan* (a prayer quorum consisting of a minimum of 10 men) because certain prayers may only be recited, and the *Torah* scroll read, in the presence of a *minyan*. If this is impossible, for whatever reason, the individual is still obliged to recite the prayers at home or work.

Tallit and tefillin

The adult male is also commanded to wear the prayer shawl or *tallit* every day and the phylacteries or *tefillin* on weekdays at morning prayer. The commandment to wear the *tallit* derives from Numbers 15: 37–41, where the children of Israel are commanded to wear fringes on the corners of their garments. Originally it was customary to wear robes which had four corners and therefore by their nature required the fringes (*tzitzit*). When the Jews moved to Western lands and adopted a different style of clothing, the rabbis of the time suggested that the men should wear a four-cornered garment for prayer so that the *mitzvah* of fringes should not be forgotten. Some Jews also wear a small *tallit* under their normal clothes so that they are fulfilling the commandment to have fringes in the corners of their garments all through the day, not just at times of prayer.

The commandment of *tefillin* is mentioned four times in the *Torah*, Exodus 13: 9 and 13: 16, Deuteronomy 6: 8 and 11: 18. In each case, there is an injunction to have 'these words' bound upon the hand and between the eyes as a sign and this is taken literally, so that the four passages are written out on parchment and placed into two small boxes, one for the head and one for the arm. Straps are attached to the boxes and can then be fastened round the head and wound round the arm. The basic idea behind this commandment is that the word of God should be carried on the arm near to the heart and on the head near the brain as a reminder to use the emotions and intellect in God's service throughout the day. The meditation often found in prayer books for use before the *tefillin* are put on encapsulates beautifully the various ideas to which this *mitzvah* gives expression: that one *tefillah* is put on the hand as a reminder of God's outstretched hand that redeemed the Jews from Egypt and opposite the heart as a reminder that all the thoughts and desires of the heart should be subjected to God's service, and one *tefillah* is put on the head near the brain as a reminder that the soul and all strength and endeavours should also be committed to the service of God.

It is customary for men to cover their heads as a sign of respect before God. For the less traditional, this will be done only in the synagogue; for the more traditional, at times of religious activity such as praying, eating or studying; and for the very traditional, at all times.

There are no other forms of dress which are a requirement of Judaism but there are certain groups who adopt distinctive dress, particularly certain Hasidic groups who wear clothes derived from 18th century Polish court dress. In general, non-traditional women do not distinguish themselves in dress from the general population but Orthodox women will usually dress modestly, although the interpretation of what is 'modest' varies considerably. Some married women also cover their hair at all times, again for 'modesty', either with a wig or a scarf; others cover their hair only when they go out of their own homes and yet others only when they go to synagogue or light *Shabbat* candles.

Limmud haTorah

Study of the *Torah* is a central activity in the life of Jews and one of the deepest forms of spiritual expression available to them. The *Torah*, in the limited sense of the five books of Moses, is for the Orthodox Jew the direct revelation of God; and to the Progressive Jew is divinely inspired. Study is a means of encounter with the divine will as expressed in revelation, a way in which people can come closer to God, and the most sacred ritual of Judaism. It is also a means to an end because *Torah*, God's instruction or teaching, is intended to be put into practice and to form the basis of all aspects of life; one must therefore study it in order to implement it. Several statements of the rabbis show the centrality of study – study of *Torah* is seen as the most important commandment because it leads to the others; in other words, true study of the will of God must by its nature lead to its implementation.

Study may take very different forms. In order to ensure a certain minimum, it is incorporated into the daily liturgy through selections from rabbinic literature which form part of the prayers and through the weekly readings from the *Torah* in the synagogue. Individuals may then study alone on a regular basis, or may go to *shiurim*, study sessions run by the local community, or may even be involved in full-time Jewish study at a *yeshiva*, an institute of higher Jewish learning. Some people belong to a *daf yomi* study group, which is a group of individuals who study a page a day from the *Talmud* or *Mishnah* and come together to celebrate the completion of each tractate or section. To study the entire *Talmud* at the rate of a page a day takes roughly seven years. One of the main features of Jewish study is that it is interactive – if possible, one should not study alone but with a companion and this is the method used in most *yeshivot*. It is known as ḥevruta and involves the class being divided up into groups of two who then look at the text to be studied and discuss and debate its implications with each other before joining together with the whole class to go through it again with the teacher. Even if it is not possible to study with someone else, the traditional way of printing the central texts of Jewish thought, with the text surrounded by commentaries of different rabbinic scholars, ensures that students are confronted by several ways of looking at every passage and must make their own response to them.

Gemilut Ḥasadim

The first area of individual life that we looked at covered human beings' communication with God; the second the ways in which they can attempt to explore God's will and nature as revealed through the *Torah*. The third area that we will examine concerns relationships with fellow humans. *Torah* demands a whole range of practices whose purpose can most easily be understood as sanctification of daily life. Just as importantly, it also inculcates particular ways of relating to others. The famous story of Hillel and Shammai, two of the rabbis of the *Mishnah* who lived in the 1st century B.C.E., bears this out. A man who wished to become a convert came to Shammai and demanded to be taught the whole of the *Torah* while he stood on one leg. Shammai refused to have anything to do with him so the man came to Hillel and put the same request to him. Hillel's response was 'That which is hateful to you, do not do to your neighbour. That is the whole of *Torah*; the rest is commentary, now go and study it.' (Babylonian *Talmud*, Shabbat 31a) The biblical verse on which that statement is based, 'you shall love your fellow as yourself' (Leviticus 19: 18), has been interpreted in Jewish tradition as not simply having loving thoughts towards our neighbours but as acting in a loving way.

Gemilut Ḥasadim may be translated as 'performing acts of benevolence' and is one of the few areas of ritual practice to which no limit is set: in other words, one can never say 'I've been kind to enough people today'. It is also something we can all do, because even someone who has no money and cannot give charity can perform kindly actions; and it can be shown to everyone, unlike charity which can only be given to the poor. It involves such practical actions as visiting the sick, hospitality to travellers, comforting mourners, attending to the dead, caring for the disadvantaged

and so on but also demands sympathy and compassion (*raḥmanut*) for the needs of others. The emphasis placed on such activities leads many Jews to be involved in caring work of all kinds, whether professionally or voluntarily.

Another practical result of the commandment to love others is the importance of charity. The Hebrew term for charity is *tzedaḵah* which comes from a root meaning 'justice' or 'righteousness'. The development of this concept shows that in Judaism giving money to those in need of it is a duty and an outworking of justice, and to receive it is a right of the poor. Many Jews follow the custom of giving a tenth of their income for charitable purposes, although it is laid down that one should not give more than a fifth so as not to impoverish oneself. Before most festive occasions, many Jews will make a contribution to charity, and certain festivals, such as *Shabbat*, the High Holydays, *Purim* and *Pesaḥ*, are particularly connected with this practice. Rabbinic sources detail the ways in which charity should be given – Maimonides, for instance, states eight degrees of charity, the highest of which is to give money to prevent another from being poor by establishing him in a job. The rabbis also emphasise the need to combine *tzedaḵah* with *raḥmanut* so that the dignity and sensitivities of the poor person are respected at all times.

Family life

Introduction

The family is the centre of much of Jewish life and is fundamental to the maintenance and transmission of the Jewish heritage. The home is often referred to as a *Miḵdash Me'at* or little sanctuary; that is to say, the home, rather than the synagogue, is seen as having become the centre of Jewish religious life after the destruction of the Temple. By this metaphor, the table around which the family eats becomes the equivalent of the Temple altar. This powerful symbolism indicates the importance to Judaism of the life of the family within the home and we will see that many religious practices can only be carried out fully within the home context.

Obviously, each family, exactly as each individual does, must make its own response to the traditions of Judaism. Practices vary widely from family to family, whether because of particular family customs derived from the area of origin of that family or because of ideological differences. Some families may also vary their behaviour at different times, according to the age and number of family members and their needs and circumstances.

The borderline between family and community is very fluid. There are many 'family' events which are celebrated by the community as well, whether they take place in the home, the synagogue or elsewhere. Communities are often very close-knit and even where the families are not interrelated, the community becomes a kind of extended family.

There are several symbols which identify a Jewish home, the most important of which is the *mezuzah*. The word literally means a doorpost and it refers to the verse in Deuteronomy 6: 9, 'and you shall write them (i.e. these words) on the doorposts of your house and on your gates'. The words referred to are, of course, the words of the *Shema* telling Israel that God is One and that Jews are commanded to love him. The words of the *Shema* are written out on a parchment and placed inside a small box which is then nailed to the right-hand doorpost of each door in the house. Some Jews will reach up a hand to the *mezuzah* every time they pass through a door and then kiss their fingers as a concrete reminder that the life of the family in the house should be lived in accordance with the ideals embodied in the words of the *Shema*. The *mezuzah* also symbolises God's protection of the house. The word *Shaddai* (Almighty) is written on the back of the parchment and it is also said to stand for the initial letters of **SH**omer *Daltot Israel* (the Guardian of the Doors of Israel). Other symbols commonly found in Jewish homes include the *Mizraḥ*, a picture or a plaque on the wall indicating the direction in which Jerusalem lies and hence the direction in which one should face in order to recite certain of the prayers, particularly the 'Amidah. The *Shiviti* may also be found in some homes. Its name derives from the verse in the Psalms 'I have kept (*shiviti*) the Lord before me always' (Psalm 16: 8) and it usually takes the form of an abstract pattern made from verses of the Bible with God's name in the centre. It is seen as a reminder of God's presence. Some very religious families also maintain the custom of leaving a small corner of a room undecorated as a permanent symbol of mourning for the destruction of the Temple in 70 C.E. and also as a symbol of the temporary nature of our material possessions.

Kashrut

The laws governing what kind of food may be eaten and how it is to be eaten play a large part in the religious expression of the Orthodox Jew. Reform and Progressive Jews tend to observe the laws at very widely differing levels and many Jewish secularists do not observe them at all, perhaps retaining only a loyalty to 'kosher-style' food. For the Orthodox Jew, eating is a ritual activity which is charged with religious meaning and is therefore governed by a complex pattern of *mitzvot*.

The basic laws of *kashrut* (a word which means 'fitness' and from which the adjective *kasher*, 'fit, proper' is derived) are to be found mainly in Leviticus, chapter 11. The *Torah* states in Genesis 1: 29 that all kinds of vegetables and plants may be eaten freely but it is not until the time of Noah that the eating of meat is permitted and it is then hedged around with conditions and restrictions. In fact, there is a tradition of Jewish vegetarianism which sees the eating of animals as a concession to human weakness and by no means as an ideal. Leviticus specified the species of animals which may be eaten: they must have cloven hooves and chew the cud. The pig is therefore forbidden because it has a cloven hoof but does not chew the cud and animals like rabbits and hares are forbidden because they chew the cud but do not have a cloven hoof. In the case of aquatic creatures, they must have fins and scales. Types of fish such as plaice or herring are *kasher* but shark, which has fins but not scales, and shellfish, which have neither, are not acceptable. Most domestic birds can be eaten but no bird which eats carrion can be used for food. All insects are also forbidden. Animal by-products such as milk and eggs can be used only if they come from a *kasher* species, so camel milk or ostrich eggs are not *kasher*.

In addition to the laws about the kind of meat which may be eaten, there are laws about how the animal is to be slaughtered. There are two areas of concern here: the general principle that the suffering caused to the animal by slaughtering should be kept to the minimum possible, and the oft-reiterated command not to eat the blood of the animal because the life of the animal is in the blood. The process of slaughter is called *sheḥitah* and must be carried out by a *shoḥet*, a slaughterer who is thoroughly versed in the minutiae of this particular area of religious law. A blessing must be recited before the act of slaughter. The animal must be killed by a single stroke of an extremely sharp knife so that the veins and arteries of the neck are instantly severed and death is virtually instantaneous. The animal is then examined to make sure that it was healthy and that there were no defects in the major organs of the body; certain parts of the carcass are removed, particularly some of the fat and the sciatic nerve (in accordance with Genesis 32: 32), both of which are forbidden. In some communities, the sciatic nerve will be carefully removed, an extremely complicated procedure known as porging, but in many others, this is not done and the hindquarters are therefore not used for *kasher* meat. The meat must then be soaked in water, salted and rinsed in order to remove as much blood as possible from it, and is then ready for use.

A further consideration is the prohibition against mixing milk and meat. The verse 'You shall not boil a kid in the milk of its mother' occurs three times in the *Torah* and on the principle that there are no wasted words in the *Torah*, the rabbis of the *Mishnah* and *Talmud* record the interpretation that something slightly different is meant each time the verse is written. The commandment is therefore threefold; milk and meat should not be cooked together, the resulting mixture should not be eaten nor should any benefit be derived from it. In an Orthodox household, rigorous precautions are taken to make sure that milk foods do not come into contact with meat: there will be two sets of crockery, cutlery, pots and pans, washing up bowls and tea towels, one set for milk foods and one for meat. After eating meat, an interval of time is observed before milk foods can be eaten (commonly three hours, though some communities keep six hours and some only one). Milk foods may be followed by meat foods, as milk is generally more quickly digested, but only after cleaning the mouth and hands.

The way in which food is eaten is seen as a form of religious expression, just as are the regulations on what is to be eaten and the way in which it is to be prepared. Before and after eating any kind of food, an appropriate blessing is recited. Before the eating of bread, the hands are washed and the blessing for bread 'Blessed are you, Lord our God, King of the Universe, who brings bread out of the earth' is recited. This then requires the recital of the full *Birkat haMazon* (Grace after Meals) when the meal is finished. The analogy of the Temple is carried through even here – when saying the blessing over bread, it is usual to sprinkle a little salt over the bread just as salt was offered with all the Temple sacrifices, and when saying *Birkat haMazon*, many people have the custom of removing all the knives from the table because no metal knives were allowed on the altar.

Another way in which food is used for religious expression is the custom of *Se'udat Mitzvah*. At many occasions where a *mitzvah* is carried out,

such as a wedding, a *Brit Milah* (circumcision), a *Pidyon haBen* (redeeming firstborn son from Temple service), the dedication of a house, or a *Bar/Bat Mitzvah*, it is usual to have a special meal to mark the event preceded by the blessing over bread and concluded by *Birkat haMazon*, often with additions which refer to the event that the meal celebrates.

Family events and rites of passage

There are many states of life and moments of transition from one stage to another which are marked by particular rituals within the Jewish religion. There may be elements of celebration, of recognition for the individual and, of course, of recognition of God's role in the life of the individual.

Birth

The birth of a child is a fulfilment of the first commandment given to humanity: in the Book of Genesis, Adam and Eve were commanded to 'be fruitful and increase' (Genesis 1: 28) and the minimum requirement for this commandment is to replace oneself, that is, for a couple to have at least two children, a boy and a girl. Obviously, not every couple is able or wishes to have children but there is a great emphasis on the importance of continuity and maintenance of Jewish traditions which can most easily come about through the transmission of Jewish values to one's children. Another imperative often found is the survival of the Jews in a century in which one third of the Jewish people were murdered. There is considerable concern among Jewish demographers that the numbers of world Jewry are continually declining. This is taken, particularly by more Orthodox Jews, as a further motivation for having several children.

There are no particular rituals associated with the moment of birth, although it is usual for the woman to recite the blessing of thanksgiving, which is used after recovery from an illness or escape from danger, at some time after the birth when she is in the presence of a *minyan*, the quorum of 10 required for community prayer.

Every child born of a Jewish mother is Jewish, without the need for any rite of initiation. A boy will, however, be circumcised after birth. This has been a religious duty since the time of Abraham (Genesis 17: 10–12) as a sign of the covenant (*Brit*) between God and the Jewish people, hence the name for the circumcision ceremony, *Brit Milah* or covenant of circumcision. It is seen primarily as a physical, outward, sign and reminder of the covenant rather than as a rite of initiation – a woman is a full member of the Jewish community without circumcision, as is a man who for medical reasons cannot be circumcised, for instance, a haemophiliac. It is a requirement for a male convert to undergo circumcision or, if he is already circumcised, to have a symbolic circumcision by shedding a drop of blood from the penis. This is again primarily as a sign of the covenant rather than an initiation ceremony since the idea that the individual is re-born as a Jew underlies the rites of conversion; therefore the convert is obliged to be circumcised just as a newborn boy is.

The ceremony of *Brit Milah* must take place on the eighth day after the birth, whether that is a weekday, a *Shabbat* or a festival, so long as the child is healthy. If there is a medical reason for delaying the circumcision, it will take place as soon as possible but not on *Shabbat* or a festival. It can take place anywhere that is most convenient – at home if the mother and baby are there, in the hospital or occasionally in the synagogue. If possible, the ceremony should take place in the presence of a *minyan*. The ceremony is usually performed by a *mohel* or circumciser who has been trained in the requirements of *Halakhah* and medical hygiene. As the ceremony is in essence a religious one, it should not be performed by an ordinary doctor. Originally the father was required to circumcise his son but it is now seen to be better to have it done by someone with more practice. Another role in the ceremony is that of the *sandek* who holds the child on his lap for the circumcision itself. It is considered an honour to be asked to be the *sandek*; often, a respected older relative will be asked to fulfil this function. A later development, most often found among Ashkenazi Jews, is that of having a *kvatter* and a *kvatterin* whose function it is to bring the child from the mother to the room in which the circumcision will take place. Elijah, the ninth century B.C.E. prophet, is also said to attend every circumcision and a special chair, known as the *kiseh shel Eliyahu*, is set aside for him.

On the morning of the circumcision, after the morning prayers have been recited, the *kvatterin* brings the child from the mother to the room in which the circumcision will take place. The *kvatter* takes the baby from the *kvatterin* while those assembled welcome the child. The baby is placed momentarily on the chair of Elijah and then on the lap of the *sandek*. The *mohel* recites a blessing before performing the circumcision and the father recites one immediately afterwards, blessing God who has commanded us to bring the child into the covenant of Abraham. Those present respond 'As this child has entered the covenant, so may he enter into the *Torah*, the marriage canopy and into good deeds.' The name of the child is also announced. At the conclusion of the ceremony, wine is drunk and a drop is given to the baby.

The birth of a daughter is marked by fewer ceremonials and there is no circumcision. In Orthodox families, the birth is publicly acknowledged by the father being called up to read the *Torah* in the synagogue soon after the birth. After the *Torah* portion has been read, a special prayer is recited for the health of the mother and baby and the Hebrew name of the child is announced. Particularly in America, some attempts have been made to devise ceremonies which will give some more public recognition of the arrival of a daughter but, as yet, there is no one accepted ritual. Among Progressive Jews, apart from the circumcision of male children, both boys and girls will be brought to the synagogue on a *Shabbat* not long after the birth for a baby blessing – the parents bring the baby forward to the *Aron haKodesh* where the scrolls of *Torah* are kept. Prayers are then recited for the welfare of the baby and the mother, and the Priestly Blessing (Numbers 6: 24–26) is recited over the baby.

Names

Every Jew has a Hebrew name, in addition to the name by which they are known for general purposes. This name is announced in the synagogue (for a girl) or at the *Brit* (for a boy) and is used in the synagogue when the person is called up to the *Torah* or when special prayers are said on their behalf and in any religious documents relating to them, for instance a marriage or divorce document. The Hebrew name consists of the given name and the name of the father and in some cases also the name of the mother, for instance *Sarah bat Yirmiyahu*, Sarah, the daughter of Jeremy or *Ya'akov Yosef ben Kalman*, Jacob Joseph, the son of Kalman.

There are many different customs surrounding naming: some, particularly Ashkenazi Jews, will call a child after a dead and honoured relative and will therefore avoid using the name of a living relative for a new baby; some, particularly Sefardi Jews, prefer to honour living relatives by using

35

their name for the child. Some use the Hebrew name as their secular given name; some have names whose meanings are related, for instance *Aryeh* (lion) for the Hebrew and Leo (Latin for lion) for the secular name; some have names that simply sound similar, for instance *Yehudit* for the Hebrew and Julia for the secular; and some have names that bear no relation to each other at all.

Pidyon haBen

Another commandment associated with the birth of children is the requirement to redeem a first-born son. The firstborn male child was originally dedicated to service in the Temple, a privilege which was transferred to the tribe of Levi after the episode of the golden calf and substituted by the requirement to redeem the child. The redemption is effected by the father paying a *kohen,* a descendant of the priestly family, five silver coins. The ceremony itself is very brief. When the child is 31 days old, the father invites a *kohen* to a feast at which the *kohen* holds the child and the father places the five coins in front of him. The *kohen* recites a formula asking whether the father would prefer to have his firstborn son or the five coins. The father always replies that he wants his child and, taking him, gives the *kohen* the money and recites the appropriate blessings. The *kohen* then recites the priestly blessing over the child. The ceremony is only necessary if neither of the child's parents are themselves descendants of the priestly or levitical families and if the firstborn is a son. If the first child is a daughter or if the birth was a caesarian or followed the miscarriage of a baby of more than three months gestation, the ceremony is not performed. Unlike the *Brit Milah,* it is a ceremony which is rarely performed by non-Orthodox Jews.

Family relations

The responsibility for children does not end with the ceremonies surrounding birth. Jewish tradition makes demands on the parents and on the children that ensure that their relationship is one of mutual respect and responsibility. Parents have an obligation to educate their children, to transmit Jewish values to them and to help them become individuals in their own right. In the *Talmud*, these obligations are expressed as a parent's duty to teach the children *Torah,* to teach them a trade and how to swim – presumably a person competent in all three areas will be able to cope with whatever life sends.

Children are commanded to honour their parents. This does not mean that they have to obey everything their parents tell them without question but that they should respect them and what they have to teach. This respect should be extended to include older members of the community, teachers and rabbis as well. Children are also expected to care for their parents, particularly in their old age.

Bar/Bat Mitzvah

When a girl reaches the age of 12 and a boy the age of 13 they become adults in the eyes of the Jewish religion and fully responsible for their own actions. Originally, the child was counted as an adult at the point when the secondary sexual characteristics appeared but it became usual to assign a standard age to it, so that all girls automatically become *Bat Mitzvah* (daughter of the commandment) at 12 and all boys are *Bar Mitzvah* (son of the commandment) at 13. The attainment of religious majority is therefore an involuntary step but it has become customary to mark it with a celebration to symbolise the voluntary and adult acceptance of God's *Torah* and the commandments.

It is a family celebration, because it marks the end of the first stage in the education of the Jew which brings him or her to a point where he or she has sufficient knowledge to carry out all the commandments on an equal footing with other adults. It also marks an acceptance of the Jewish values which the family has attempted to transmit through its living out of the principles of *Torah*. It is also to some extent a community celebration because a new adult member of the community is being welcomed into his or her full rights and duties.

As the main significance of *Bar/Bat Mitzvah* is that the child now becomes fully responsible for fulfilling the *mitzvot* of the *Torah,* the main ceremonial is associated with the *Torah*. At a service on a day when the *Torah* is read – a Monday, a Thursday, a Sabbath, a festival or a New Moon – the boy is called up (given an 'Aliyah, literally a going-up) to the reading of the *Torah*. This symbolises his acceptance of the *Torah* and the covenant and celebrates his attainment of the full rights and duties of an adult Jew. His father formally declares that his son is now responsible for his own actions. The celebration is held as soon as possible after the 13th birthday according to the Hebrew calendar. Very often, the boy, apart from having his own 'Aliyah (generally the last, which carries with it the privilege of reciting the *Haftarah,* the prophetical portion as well), chants the whole of the *Torah* portion for that week; a considerable achievement as the handwritten scrolls of *Torah* used in the synagogue do not have the vowel pointings or the musical notation normally found in the printed text of the Hebrew Bible. He may also lead some part of the morning service. As is customary with many events in Jewish life, it is usual for there to be a special meal after the service at which the boy might give a *D'var Torah,* an exposition and commentary on some words of *Torah.*

The celebration of a *Bat Mitzvah* is much less standardised. Within Orthodox Judaism, the different religious role and responsibilities of the woman are reflected by their attainment being marked in a different way. Because the woman does not take a public role in religious services, it would be inappropriate for her to lead part of the service or to be called up to the reading of the *Torah,* although in America there is a growing trend among Orthodox Jews to have 'women only' services for a *Bat Mitzvah* at which the girl is called up to the reading of the *Torah* in exactly the same way as her brother. In England, the more usual pattern is for a group of 12-year-old girls to prepare a *D'var Torah* which is given at a later point in the service or at the *Kiddush* after the end of the service. In the Progressive movement, the celebration of a *Bar Mitzvah* at the age of 13 was abandoned in the early years of the movement in favour of a confirmation for both boys and girls at the age of 16 on the grounds that 13 was too young for a conscious acceptance of adult obligations. The group celebration of confirmation, often at the time of the festival of *Shavuot,* as a form of graduation from religion school has been retained, particularly by Liberal congregations, but *Bar/Bat Mitzvah* has crept back into favour. Usually no distinction is made by Progressive Jews between the ways in which a *Bar Mitzvah* and a *Bat Mitzvah* are celebrated. In fact, the first *Bat Mitzvah* ceremony was performed in 1922 by Judith Kaplan, the daughter of the founder of the Reconstructionist movement in America.

Marriage

Jewish beliefs about human nature and relationships are reflected in the attitude to and practices surrounding the marriage relationship. Marriage is seen as an ideal and, indeed, a positive duty. This can be seen throughout *Torah* but of course particularly in the commandments given to Adam and Eve in Genesis 1: 28 and 2: 24 and again to Noah in Genesis 9: 7. The word used for marriage, *kiddushin,* which derives from the root *kadosh* meaning 'holy', gives some indication of the centrality and importance of marriage to Judaism.

The way in which a marriage partner is chosen varies enormously from community to community and depends on the level of traditionalism of the prospective partners. Very traditional Jews may well have their marriages arranged, as the opportunities for free socialisation between the sexes are relatively restricted. The marriage broker or *shadhan* will attempt to match the families and their expectations as well as the couple themselves. Other Jews will meet and court their partners very much as their non-Jewish peers do, although the observant will in general bear in mind restrictions on pre-marital sexual relations. Nearly all Jewish parents, even the non-observant, will hope and expect that their children will find a Jewish partner. Because of the extraordinary importance of the family in transmitting Jewish values, it is recognised that it would be very difficult to live a Jewish family life if one of the partners is not Jewish. There is also the practical problem that, according to the *Halakhah,* the children of a Jewish wife and a non-Jewish father are Jewish whereas the children of a non-Jewish wife and a Jewish father are not. 'Mixed' marriages can therefore cause problems of personal status for Orthodox Jews. A religious marriage ceremony cannot take place where one of the partners is not Jewish.

A betrothal ceremony or *Tena'im* only takes place in very traditional communities. It is usually held at home. A document is read aloud at the ceremony which sets out the obligations of both parties to each other, stipulates the amount of the dowry and specifies certain penalties for breaking off the engagement.

The wedding ceremony itself can take place only on certain days – days which are not permitted include the Sabbath, festivals, fast days, the period of semi-mourning between *Pesah* and *Shavuot* and the three weeks leading up to the fast of the ninth of Av. On the Sabbath before the wedding, the groom will be called up to the reading of the *Torah* in his own or his parents' synagogue, a ceremony known in Yiddish, the vernacular of Ashkenazi Jews, as an *aufruf.* The bride and groom do not see each other for a period preceding the wedding, and will usually fast before the wedding ceremony itself, because the wedding is seen as a new stage of life where one begins afresh and one's previous sins are forgiven as they are on *Yom Kippur*. Similarly, it is customary for the bride to wear white, to symbolise purity. In some more Orthodox families, the groom wears a *kittel*, a white garment also worn on *Yom Kippur*.

The wedding can take place anywhere, not necessarily in the synagogue. For some Jews it is traditional to marry in the open air beneath the sky to symbolise the hope that the progeny of the couple will be as numerous as the stars. Immediately before the wedding, the bridegroom will be taken to the room in which the bride is waiting and he will cover her face with her veil. The reason usually cited for this ceremony, known as *bedeken*, is so that he will see her face and know that he is getting married to the right bride, unlike Jacob with Leah (Genesis 29: 25), but the main reason is so that the groom or the rabbi can recite the blessing of Rebecca, 'Our sister, may you become the mother of myriads' (Genesis 24: 60). The groom is then accompanied by his father and father-in-law to the place where the ceremony will take place. They stand beneath a canopy or *ḥuppah* which may be an elaborate velvet canopy or simply a large *tallit* supported by a pole at each corner. It symbolises the future home of the couple. The bride then enters, accompanied by her mother and mother-in-law, and walks around the groom a certain number of times. The interpretations for this custom differ, as do the number of encirclements. The most common explanation and number is seven times because the words 'and when a man takes a wife' occur seven times in *Torah*. It also symbolises the bride entering the seven spheres of her husband's soul. The bride then stands on the groom's right and their parents stand beside them. In some cases, the siblings also stand with them so that the couple marry surrounded by their whole family.

There are two parts to the marriage ceremony, both of which are quite brief. The first part, *Ḳiddushin* or sanctification, begins with the recital of the betrothal blessings, *Birkhot Erusin*. These are two blessings recited over a cup of wine by the person who is performing the ceremony. In fact, this person does not strictly speaking perform the ceremony – the groom does that – but he is known as *mesader Ḳiddushin* which is probably most accurately translated as the marriage facilitator. Next comes the core ritual which brings about the marriage – the groom hands his wife a ring which should be of a certain minimum value and of plain metal so that she should not be deceived about its worth, and recites the formula 'Be sanctified

(*mekudeshet*) to me with this ring in accordance with the laws of Moses and Israel'. The ring is placed on the bride's index finger so that it can be clearly seen. This must be done in the presence of two male witnesses. Next, to mark the division between the two parts of the ceremony, the *ketuba* or marriage document is read aloud, usually in its original Aramaic, the vernacular used by Jews at the time of the *Mishnah* and *Talmud*. The *ketuba* will have been signed immediately before the ceremony by two male witnesses and sets out the duties and obligations of the husband. It is an extremely business-like document and enumerates the rights of the wife to a certain level of care and maintenance during the marriage and specifies her right to support after the marriage, whether it ends through death or divorce. Many couples have a beautifully illuminated or decorated *ketuba*.

The second part is known as *Nissuin* which was originally performed at a later date but now follows on immediately after the *Ḳiddushin*. This consists of the bride receiving the *ketuba*, and the recital of the *Birkhot Nissuin* under the *ḥuppah*. These are the marriage blessings which are seven in number and are therefore also known as *Sheva Berakhot*, the seven blessings. Again, they are recited over a cup of wine. The final moment of the ceremony is for the bridegroom to stamp on a wine glass and shatter it as a reminder of the destruction of the Temple in Jerusalem, so that even in this moment of joy, there is a slight note of sadness. As soon as he has done that, all present call out *mazal tov*, good luck, and the main ceremony is over. Before the *Se'udat Mitzvah*, however, the bride and groom must retire to a private room for a few minutes. This *yiḥud*, being alone together, symbolises their new relationship because it is not usual for traditional Jews to be alone in a room with a member of the opposite sex. In fact, the time alone is generally used by the couple to break their fast. The *Se'udat Mitzvah* or festive meal is concluded with a special *Birkat haMazon* at which the *Sheva Berakhot* are again recited, and the celebrations conclude with dancing. It is a positive injunction to cause the bride and the groom to rejoice on their wedding and this is done with circle dances, singing and entertainment. For the week after the wedding, the bride and groom may continue to celebrate at special meals to which people who could not be present at the wedding will be invited and at which the *Birkhat haMazon* and *Sheva Berakhot* will be recited. This custom is generally followed only by more traditional families as other Jews have begun to follow the Western custom of leaving soon after the wedding for a honeymoon.

Although relations between the sexes are restricted before marriage, especially in traditional communities, marital sexual relations are encouraged. They are seen as the husband's duty and the wife's right, and the *Talmud* even specifies the number of times a week the wife can expect her husband to have sex with her, depending on his profession. Obviously, one of the purposes of sexual relations is procreation but the other purposes of companionship and pleasure are acknowledged and seen as equally legitimate. On the other hand, because of the laws of family purity, the couple are also enabled to see their relationship not purely in sexual terms but can and must communicate on other levels as well. The *Torah* forbids sexual relations between a husband and his menstruating wife, who must count a certain number of days for the menstrual flow and then a further period of seven days in which there is no bleeding before going to the ritual bath or *mikveh* and resuming sexual relations with her husband. During this time, the couple do not sleep together and have no intimate contact with each other and therefore have to use channels of communication other than sexual ones; their sexual relationship also maintains an element of freshness and rediscovery each month. The *mikveh* is a specially constructed bath that uses 'living' waters, that is, rain water or a natural source of water rather than tap water; and is used purely as a ritual bath. In fact, the woman actually bathes in an ordinary tub before using the *mikveh*, so it would be mistaken to see the *mikveh* purely as a form of hygiene and to regard menstruation as 'unclean'. However, perhaps because of the very private nature of this area of life, it is probably a minority of Orthodox Jews who keep the laws of family purity in their entirety. The Progressive movements have in general abandoned all the categories of ritual purity and impurity as a relic of Temple times with no relevance for the religious life of the modern Jew.

Birth control is a possibility for Jews on grounds of health, particularly once the basic requirements of *p'ru u r'vu*, be fruitful and increase, have been fulfilled by having at least two children, a boy and a girl. However, certain methods of contraception are not permitted, particularly where they involve the spilling of seed, the sin for which Onan was condemned in the *Torah*. *Coitus interruptus* and the use of the condom are therefore not permitted. The use of the I.U.D. is also questioned because its efficacy may depend on it being a very early abortifacient. Methods such as the Pill, so long as they do not damage the health of the woman and do not cause intra-menstrual bleeding, are accepted by many halakhic authorities, although there are groups, particularly among the very traditional, who regard children as a blessing from God and would not use contraception, except in cases where life would otherwise be endangered.

Abortion is not normally encouraged. It is, however, not equated with murder and the mother's health takes precedence so that if the pregnancy would be life-threatening for the mother, abortion is encouraged to save her. The problems come in determing what is a life- or health-threatening pregnancy for a mother and the halakhic sources contain a great range of rulings on this subject, depending on the particular situation of the mother.

The ideal for marriage in Judaism is for it to last throughout life but it is also acknowledged that this ideal cannot always apply. If a marriage breaks, divorce is permitted in Jewish tradition. The *ketuba* that the husband signed at the wedding provides for the rights of the wife in the event of divorce, although in practice nowadays in Western countries, the Talmudic principle of 'the law of the country is the law' takes precedence and it is usual for there to have been a civil divorce before the religious divorce, which will take care of such matters as maintenance and division of property. However, before the partners are free to marry again, the husband must give his wife a *get* or divorce document which dissolves their relationship. Once the *get* has been given, both partners can marry again in a religious ceremony exactly as before. The only problems in this area arise when the husband has disappeared or refuses to give the *get*, because he, not his wife, has to effect the divorce, although he is prevented by rabbinic law from divorcing her against her will. There are certain sanctions that the rabbinical courts can apply to an unwilling husband but a missing husband is much more problematical and sometimes leads to cases of *agunah,* a woman who is still bound to her husband and would be entering an adulterous relationship if she married anyone else. This area is one of the major issues of contention between the Orthodox and Progressive Jews. Orthodox rabbis make all attempts possible to help an *agunah* within the framework of *Halakhah* but are sometimes unable to help the woman further, whereas Progressive rabbis use methods of annulling a marriage retroactively which are unacceptable to the Orthodox. This then means that if a woman who has obtained a divorce

under the auspices of a Progressive rabbi re-
marries, the new relationship will be considered
adulterous by the Orthodox and the children of it
mamzerim or bastards and subject to considerable
disadvantages.

Death and dying

Jewish teaching about death and life after death
tends not to go beyond general assertions that
there is life after death and that God will judge
each soul for its actions in life. There are few
detailed theological expositions of exactly what
that life or judgement will consist of. This is partly
because it is seen as more or less impossible for us
to grasp the nature of *haOlam haBa,* the World to
Come, and partly because our primary task is to
fulfil the *mitzvot* in this world and not to speculate
about the World to Come. There are different
views expressed on the relative status of each
world. For instance, Rabbi Jacob in *The Sayings of
the Fathers,* a second century work, says 'One hour
of repentance and good deeds in this life is better
than the whole life of the World to Come but one
hour of spiritual bliss in the World to Come is
better than the whole of this life' (Avot 4: 22).
Judaism places value both on this world, seeing
life as good in itself and a unique opportunity for
serving God, and on the World to Come, because
this world is not seen as the end but as a
preparation for the World to Come.

These beliefs about life after death are reflected
in the particular practices surrounding death and
dying. There is great concern for the dying person
while they are still alive. When they die, the focus
is almost entirely on the bereaved because the soul
of the dead person is in God's hands, though the
physical remains must be treated with respect
(*K'vod haMet*).

It is considered a great *mitzvah,* commandment,
to care for the sick, to visit them and to look after
their needs. A dying person will therefore be given
all possible comfort and care, whether by
members of the family or the community. It is
forbidden to hasten the moment of death. For
example, the rabbis compare even an action as
gentle as closing the eyes of a dying person to
touching a guttering candle and thereby causing it
to go out. When it is obvious that death is
approaching, the dying person should recite the
Viddui or confession which can be found in the
prayer book and, if possible, should say the first
verse of the *Shema* (Deuteronomy 6: 4) immediately
before death.

Once death has taken place, *K'vod haMet*

requires that the dead be buried with all possible
speed, preferably on the same day and certainly by
the next, because it is considered disrespectful to
leave a body unburied. Before burial, the body
must be washed, a process known as *taharah,* by
the members of the Ḥevrah Ḳadisha (literally, holy
society) who have the privilege of doing the job of
caring for the dead. The body is carefully washed
and dressed in simple shrouds, including, in the
case of a man, the *kittel,* the white garment worn on
Yom Kippur, and the *tallit.* Traditionally, no coffin is
used, but where it is required by civil law, it should
also be of simple design. Despite the speed with
which the funeral has to be arranged, the *mitzvah*
of accompanying a body to burial is taken very
seriously and people will make all efforts to attend.
Among Orthodox Jews, cremation is not permitted, because this is seen as a denial of the belief
in a bodily resurrection in the messianic age, but
Progressive Jews do practise cremation. Neither
group follows the practice of dressing the body
and displaying it in the coffin before the funeral.

The funeral service itself is brief and generally
takes place in a small building within the grounds
of the cemetery. Each Jewish community usually
consecrates and maintains its own cemetery.
Immediately before the funeral, ḳ'ri'ah or tearing
takes place. The mourners make a tear in a
garment as a symbol of their torn and broken
hearts while reciting the blessing 'Blessed be the
true judge'. At the service, psalms are recited and a
eulogy of the dead person is given. The coffin is
then carried to the graveside while Psalm 91 is
recited and, after the coffin has been lowered into
the grave, those present each throw three spade-
fuls of earth onto the coffin.

Immediately after the funeral, the mourners
return home and the period of mourning begins.
The first period of intense mourning lasts seven
days and is therefore known as *Shiva* (literally,
seven). During this time the close relatives of the
deceased (wife/husband, brother, sister, son,
daughter, mother and father) stay at the dead
person's house. As an expression of their grief,
they sit only on low stools and do not shave, wear
leather shoes or have sexual relations. They are
looked after by other relatives and friends who
ensure that they are provided with meals,
particularly the first meal that is eaten after the
return from the funeral. This is known as the
se'udat havra'ah and begins the process of healing:
symbolic foods, particularly round foods such as
eggs or lentils which indicate the full circle of life
and death and regeneration, are served. At each of
the three daily prayer services, the mourners have

to recite the *Ḳaddish*. The *Ḳaddish* prayer itself makes no mention of death or dying: it is a prayer of exultant praise of God and symbolises the fact that the dead are not truly departed so long as their own faith and belief in God is maintained by those whom they leave behind. It can only be recited in the presence of a *minyan*, so a prayer service with a minimum of 10 men is convened three times a day at their house. The only occasion on which the mourners leave the house is on *Shabbat*, when the public show of mourning is suspended. Friends and acquaintances visit the family during the *Shiva* period in order to share their grief and comfort them.

The 30 days following the funeral (the first seven days of which are covered by the *Shiva*) is a period of less intense mourning when the family will return to work but will refrain from attending parties, concerts or celebrations. For deceased brothers, sisters, spouses or children, the mourning period ends at the end of 30 days (*sh'loshim*) but for a deceased parent, mourning continues for a whole year to reflect the primacy of the relationship between a child and parent, and the force of the commandment to honour one's parents. The bereaved child will continue to say the *Ḳaddish* at daily services for a further 10 months, and will also recite it on the *yahrzeit*, the Yiddish word for anniversary of a death.

In Britain the first *yahrzeit* is also often the time at which a stone will be placed on the grave to mark the burial place of the deceased, although this can be done earlier. The stages of ritual mourning mark the gradual return of the bereaved to normal life and provide a framework for them to work through their grief, supported by other family and community members.

Family celebration

One of the major features of Judaism is the sanctification of time and the celebration of festivals in a weekly and yearly cycle. These festivals are part of the life of the community and are celebrated partly in the synagogue but, in nearly every case, are expressed more fully in the home.

Shabbat

It may seem unexpected to the non-Jew but the most important 'festival' is the Sabbath, or *Shabbat*, partly because of the emphasis on it in the *Torah*

and *Halakhah* and partly because it occurs more often than any other festival and therefore plays a significant role in shaping Jewish life.

The commandment to observe the Sabbath occurs in two versions, in the Ten Commandments as they appear in Exodus and as they appear in Deuteronomy. In the first version, the observance of *Shabbat* is associated with the creation and God's own rest on the seventh day of creation, and in the second with the slavery in Egypt and the Exodus. The Sabbath thus commemorates God's creation of the universe, God's historical relationship with the people of Israel, and the principle of social equality and compassion, 'so that your servants may rest as well as you'. These themes can all be seen in the ways in which the day is celebrated.

The main feature of *Shabbat* is the commandment to rest and do no kind of work. The written *Torah* is not very specific about the nature of work, mentioning only one or two things such as lighting fires and carrying objects through the street but the oral *Torah* enumerates in great detail 39 different categories which are covered by the Hebrew term *melakhah*, or work. They are most easily understood by referring back to the themes of *Shabbat*, particularly that of creation – on *Shabbat*, Jews abstain from purposeful use of their creative skills in order to acknowledge God as the creator and ruler of the world, and to follow the pattern set by God in the first *Shabbat*; they also celebrate their freedom to abstain from incessant labour. Observant Jews will therefore abstain from such creative activities as cooking, writing, gardening, sewing and so on, so that they can truly rest. They are cut off from their normal weekday activities and preoccupations and are free to experience an island in time, a symbol and foretaste of the messianic age of redemption. Those Jews who do not share the Orthodox attitude to revelation and do not accept the oral *Torah* as authoritative, might have other interpretations of 'work' and will therefore celebrate the Sabbath in a different way.

In preparation for *Shabbat*, all the food to be eaten on the day is bought and cooked in advance, the house is cleaned, and the family bathes and changes so that both the house and the family are ready to welcome *Shabbat*, which is often personified as a bride or a queen. The Sabbath is then inaugurated with the lighting of two candles, usually by the woman of the house, a short time before sunset. The Jewish day always starts in the evening because of the description of creation 'There was evening and morning, the first day'

(Genesis 1: 5). Because of the holiness of *Shabbat*, the indeterminate period between sunset and true dark is counted as part of the day both on Friday and on Saturday so that the day actually lasts something over 25 hours. When those members of the family who have been to the synagogue return, the father blesses each child with the words of the priestly blessing (Numbers 6: 24–26), and a song is sung to welcome the Sabbath angels who are traditionally supposed to accompany them back from the synagogue. *Kiddush,* the prayer of sanctification for the Sabbath, is then recited over a full cup of wine and the family sit down for a special meal. The meal begins with the blessing for bread on two plaited loaves known as *Hallah.* These symbolise the double portion of mannah that fell before the Sabbath during the desert wanderings of the Children of Israel (Exodus 16: 14–26). The meal itself should be the best meal of the week and it is customary to invite guests to share it. It is also customary to sing special *Shabbat* table songs, known as *zemirot,* during the meal to add to the atmosphere of peace and enjoyment. The meal is concluded with the singing of *Birkat haMazon,* the grace after meals. The atmosphere is relaxed, there is time to enjoy being with family and friends; the outside world, in the shape of telephone, television or business worries cannot intrude.

On Saturday morning, most members of the family will go to the synagogue and return for another festive meal preceded by *Kiddush,* accompanied by *zemirot* and concluded by *Birkat haMazon.* The afternoon will then be spent in study of *Torah,* often the portion read in synagogue that *Shabbat,* or with conversation, family walks in the park or any other activity consonant with the spirit of *Shabbat.*

Shabbat is concluded after nightfall with the ceremony of *Havdalah.* This marks the distinction between the Sabbath and the normal working week, between holy and mundane. It is a beautiful ceremony full of symbolism, involving the use of all five senses and also replete with messianic overtones. A specially braided candle is lit, symbolising by the lighting of fire – one of the most fundamentally creative acts – all those activities from which Jews have abstained during the Sabbath. A cup of wine is drunk and fragrant spices are smelt, as a comfort for the loss of the 'extra soul' which one is supposed to possess on *Shabbat* and which has just departed. Blessings are recited thanking God for the faculties which enable one to distinguish *Shabbat* from the rest of the week and then the candle is extinguished in a little of the wine. Everybody wishes each other *Shavua tov,* a good week, and songs looking forward to the time of redemption, a time when the Sabbath will never cease, are sung.

The calendar

All Jewish festivals, apart from *Shabbat* which falls on a particular day of the week, fall on dates which are calculated according to the Jewish calendar. This calendar differs from the secular one and works on a sophisticated system. It is calculated both according to the moon and to the sun – unlike the Christian calendar, which is purely solar, or the Muslim one, which is only lunar. The Jewish month is a moon month, beginning at the New Moon and lasting 29 or 30 days. Twelve lunar months give a year totalling 354 days, 11 days shorter than a solar year so that if no adjustment were made, the Jewish festivals would move slowly backwards against the solar year and lose the seasonal associations. There is, therefore, a system of leap years in which the last month of the year, *Adar,* is repeated every two or three years so that over 19 years, the Jewish year averages 365¼ days. This means that the dates of the Jewish festivals move about in relation to the Christian calendar although they always remain in the same season and therefore retain their links with the agricultural cycle of the land of Israel. Thus the festival of *Rosh haShanah,* the New Year, which is celebrated on the 1st and 2nd of the month *Tishri,* falls on September 9th and 10th in 1991, September 28th and 29th in 1992, September 16th and 17th in 1993 and so on.

The names of the Jewish months used now are in fact Babylonian. Some of the original Hebrew names are used in *Torah,* such as *Aviv,* the spring month now called *Nisan* (c.f. Deuteronomy 16: 1), but since the months are more generally referred to by number (c.f. Numbers 28: 17–29: 1), we do not know what all the other names were or even if they existed. The table below shows how the months correspond to the months of the Christian calendar and the seasons in Israel.

Nisan	March/April	SPRING
Iyar	April/May	
Sivan	May/June	
Tammuz	June/July	SUMMER
Av	July/August	
Ellul	August/September	
Tishri	September/October	AUTUMN
Heshvan	October/November	
Kislev	November/December	

Tevet	December/January	WINTER
Sh'vat	January/February	
Adar	February/March	

Originally, the calendar was calculated by observation and the New Moon would be announced after reliable witnesses had come to tell the Sanhedrin (Jewish court of justice) that they had seen it. Messengers would be sent out to all the Jewish communities to let them know when the New Moon had been and therefore on what day the festivals of that month should be celebrated. This system worked well for communities in Israel but communities outside Israel (the Diaspora) sometimes did not hear when the New Moon had been till after the date of the festival. The custom therefore arose in the Diaspora of celebrating each festival for two days rather than one, that is, acting as if the last month had had 29 *and* 30 days so that whichever it turned out to have been, they would have celebrated the correct day as the festival. Even after the calendar was calculated in advance so that there was no need to wait for messengers, the Diaspora communities retained the custom of two-day festivals, and the Orthodox Jews still follow this practice. The Reform and Liberal Jews have abandoned it and keep only one day as holy.

Jewish festivals can be classified into three groups. The first is that of the three pilgrim festivals, or *Shalosh Regalim,* so called because every Jew was expected to go up to the Temple in Jerusalem to celebrate them. They are *Pesah,* or Passover, (*Nisan* 15th–21st), *Shavuot* or Pentecost (*Sivan* 6th) and *Sukkot,* or Tabernacles, (*Tishri* 15th–21st). Each of these festivals has an historical and an agricultural significance. The second group are the New Year festivals, *Rosh haShanah,* New Year, (*Tishri* 1st) and *Yom Kippur,* the Day of Atonement (*Tishri* 10th). The third is that of the non–biblical minor festivals, *Ḥanukkah* (*Kislev* 25th–*Tevet* 2nd) and *Purim* (*Adar* 14th). There are also minor fasts, mostly connected with events surrounding the destruction of the Temple and some rabbinic and modern minor celebrations, such as *Tu biSh'vat,* the New Year for Trees, *Lag ba'Omer, Yom ha'Atzma'ut,* Israeli Independence Day and so on. Each New Moon (*Rosh Ḥodesh*) is also celebrated as a minor festival.

Pesaḥ

Pesaḥ is one of the most important festivals, commemorating the Exodus from Egypt and God's redemption of the Jewish people. The central features of its observance are nearly all connected in some way with the home.

In common with the other two pilgrim festivals, *Pesaḥ* has both historical and agricultural significance. The barley harvest was gathered at this time and the first fruits of the barley would have been offered at the Temple, as would the first fruits of the flocks. Since the destruction of the Temple, however, the main emphasis of the festival has been on the historical and spiritual implications of the Exodus. It commemorates redemption from slavery and freedom.

The enormous importance of the Exodus for the Jewish religion is emphasised continually. Jews are reminded of it daily in the *Shaḥarit* service; many commandments refer to it, including the first of the Ten Commandments, which links the monotheistic belief of Judaism to that act of redemption (Exodus 20: 2), and those commandments which require sensitivity to the needs of the disadvantaged, the stranger, the widow, the orphan. *Shabbat,* the day of freedom, is the weekly commemoration of the escape from slavery at the Exodus, as we are reminded in the *Ķiddush.* In order to foster this awareness of the significance of the Exodus, we are told that each Jew in every generation should feel that he or she left Egypt with Moses, experiencing themselves the misery of slavery and the joy of redemption. *Pesaḥ* is packed with concrete symbols of the Exodus, with a graphic account of how it took place and with many pædagogic devices designed to capture the interest of every member of the family.

The main principle of *Pesaḥ* observance is 'Seven days shall you eat unleavened bread (*matzah*) . . . seven days shall there be no leavened products (*Ḥametz*) found in your homes, for whoever eats *Ḥametz,* that person shall be cut off from the congregation' (Exodus 12: 15, 19). This is in commemoration of the unleavened bread that the Israelites baked in their haste to escape from Egypt (Exodus 12: 39). *Matzah* is the basic symbol of slavery – it is referred to as *leḥem 'oni,* the bread of affliction – and also the symbol of the redemption from that slavery. By eating the same food as our ancestors, we re-experience vividly their suffering in Egypt and their exultation in freedom. *Ḥametz,* leavened products, are defined as any of the five grains, wheat, barley, oats, spelt and rye, that have been in contact with water for more than 18 minutes. These are pure *Ḥametz,* and are forbidden on *Pesaḥ.* Because a minute quantity of leaven can affect large amounts of other foodstuffs, traditional Jews will also ensure that every crumb of leaven or anything into which leaven could have got, is

43

removed from the house. This requires a rigorous physical cleaning of the house, particularly the kitchen, and parallels the spiritual preparation necessary for the experience of redemption. Special foodstuffs must be bought. The kitchenware used during the year must be put away and kitchenware kept specially for *Pesaḥ* must be brought out. The oven and all areas involved in the preparation of food must be thoroughly cleaned.

On the day before the festival begins, there is a tradition that all firstborn sons should fast as a reminder that God passed over the houses of Israel so that they were saved from the last and worst plague, the Killing of the Firstborn (Exodus 12: 29).

The festival begins in the evening, after the festival candles have been lit, with the *Seder* meal. This takes place in the home – although some synagogues organise a communal *Seder* on one or both nights of the festival – and most families invite several guests so that no one will be left to celebrate *Pesaḥ* by themselves. In fact, because the *mitzvah* of hospitality is so widely practised on this night, this is the only occasion when the synagogue festival evening service does not include the recitation of *Ḳiddush*. It is expected that everyone will be going to somebody's house and will hear the *Ḳiddush* there as part of the *Seder* meal. *Seder* actually means 'order' which indicates something of the ritual nature of the meal. The book in which all the details of the procedure can be found is known as the *Hagaddah*, or 'retelling'. The highly detailed symbolism of the meal serves the central purpose of re-living the experience of slavery, exodus and redemption.

The service begins with the youngest person present asking the questions, 'Why is this night different from all other nights? Why do we eat only unleavened bread? Why do we dip a vegetable in salt water? Why do we eat bitter herbs? Why do we all sit in a reclining position as Roman freemen did?' The questions express a child's natural curiosity at all the different and unusual things that happen at *Pesaḥ* and provide the starting point for the recounting of the story: 'You shall tell your child on that day "it is because of that which the Lord did for me when I came out of Egypt"' (Exodus 13: 8). In retelling the story, the *Hagaddah* uses verses from the *Torah*, songs, Midrashic commentaries on the text of *Torah*, allegories, psalms, stories and a range of symbolic foods. Four cups of wine are drunk, which stand for God's four different acts of salvation (Exodus 6: 6–7). Unleavened bread is eaten as the bread of affliction and slavery but also as the bread of freedom. The roasted egg and roasted shankbone on the table stand for the festival and Paschal sacrifices that are no longer brought since the destruction of the Temple. Bitter herbs are eaten to symbolise the bitterness of slavery. The mixture known as *haroset*, made from apples and nuts, is eaten to symbolise the mortar used by the Israelites to make bricks in Egypt. The whole service usually takes a considerable time, as each passage is discussed, different interpretations are given and each member of the family refers to different *Hagaddah* commentaries. Much attention is also centred on the children whose interest in and awareness of the history of the Jewish people is awakened at the *Seder*. A meal is also eaten, with the usual *Birkat haMazon;* the evening concludes with traditional *Pesaḥ* songs.

Pesaḥ lasts for seven days (eight in the Diaspora) and the first and last days (first two and last two in the Diaspora) are celebrated as festivals, with the *Seder* on the first (or first two) nights. The intermediate days of the festival are known as *Ḥol haMoed,* the festive weekdays, on which a limited range of work is permitted. During the entire week, no leavened products, such as flour, bread, pasta, and for Ashkenazi Jews no rice or pulses, should be eaten, which requires considerable ingenuity in the kitchen and gives rise to a whole range of traditional recipes for *Pesaḥ* cooking.

The *Omer*

The *Omer* is a period of counting which begins on the second day of *Pesaḥ* and lasts until *Shavuot,* the Feast of Weeks which is seven weeks after *Pesaḥ*. This practice is commanded in Leviticus 23: 15, where the Israelites were told to bring the *Omer,* a sheaf of barley, to the Temple on the first day of *Pesaḥ* and to count the days and weeks from that festival to the other. The original agricultural significance of the *Omer* period diminished after the destruction of the Temple but the practice was maintained because it also had the spiritual significance of connecting the physical birth of the nation in the Exodus, which *Pesaḥ* celebrates, with its spiritual birth in the revelation at Mount Sinai, celebrated at *Shavuot*. It is now a period of semi-mourning, some say as a commemoration of a plague which decimated the school of Rabbi Akiva and some say in mourning for the Roman persecutions of the followers of Bar Kokhba. During part of this time, weddings cannot be celebrated nor may hair be cut. An exception to this is the 33rd day of the *Omer, Lag ba'Omer,* when the plague – or the persecutions – abated. In recent years, *Yom ha'Atzma'ut*, Israeli Independence Day, and *Yom Yerushalayim*, the day of the reunification of Jerusalem, both of which fall in the *Omer* period, have also been treated as exceptions; but two other recent additions to the calendar, *Yom haShoah*, Holocaust Remembrance Day, and *Yom haZikkaron*, Remembrance Day for Israel's soldiers, are in any case appropriate to the atmosphere of mourning. The actual procedure for the counting is very brief. Each evening, a blessing is recited and then the number of that day in the *Omer* is said aloud. Many people have special calendars, known as *Sefirah* counters, hung up somewhere in the house to help them remember to count and to know how far the count has got.

Shavuot

Shavuot is the second of the three pilgrim festivals and falls on the 6th of *Sivan*, on the 50th day of the *Omer* count – hence the English name, Pentecost, which derives from the Greek for 50. It tends to suffer in comparison with the other two, *Pesaḥ* and *Sukkot*. They both last for a whole week (or eight days in the Diaspora) with a festival on the first and last day, whereas *Shavuot* is only a one-day festival (or two days outside Israel) and is much less widely known outside the Jewish community. It has, however, equal depth of meaning and importance. Historically, it is the festival which celebrates the revelation at Mount Sinai, the moment when the *Torah* was revealed to the Jewish people; the culmination of the covenant between God and Israel. Agriculturally, it is the festival of First Fruits, *Ḥag haBikkurim*, when the summer wheat harvest began in Israel and the first fruits of that harvest were offered at the Temple. Since the destruction of the Temple, the historical and spiritual aspects of *Shavuot* have been emphasised much more than the agricultural ones and many customs associated with the festival, which were probably originally to do with the harvest, have been reinterpreted to refer to the historical events. For instance, it is usual to eat dairy foods, such as cheese pancakes and cheese-cakes, on *Shavuot*, a custom found in other cultures associated with harvest festivals but here given several different interpretations, all referring to the Sinai revelation.

The festival starts, as all festivals do, with the lighting of candles, *Ḳiddush* over wine and a festive meal. One special feature of *Shavuot* is that many people follow the custom of staying awake all night and studying *Torah* in preparation for the revelation in the morning. This is known as a *Tiḳḳun leil Shavuot* and usually takes the form of symbolically studying each book of the *Tanakh* by reading the first and last verses of each *parashah* of the *Torah*, the first and last verses of each prophetical book, certain Psalms and the whole of the book of Ruth, which is particularly connected to *Shavuot*, and then studying the beginning and end of each of the 63 tractates of the *Mishnah* and certain other rabbinical works. The purpose of studying all night is to show eagerness to receive *Torah*, unlike the Israelites who are supposed to have slept the night before the Revelation.

Another dimension of the festival is its connection with Jewish learning in general. Traditionally, *Shavuot* was the time when a young child would begin learning Hebrew, and it is still often taken by synagogue religion schools as an opportunity for emphasising the centrality of the *Torah* and the Covenant of Sinai for Judaism.

Sukkot

Sukkot is the third of the three pilgrim festivals, and, like the others, has a dual symbolism, historical and agricultural. Historically, it commemorates God's protection of the Jewish people in the wanderings through the desert in the 40 years after the Exodus from Egypt. It is also celebrated at the time when the final harvest of the year was gathered in Israel, so it is a festival of thanksgiving for the bounty of the land. Like *Pesaḥ*, it is celebrated for seven days (eight outside Israel) but is immediately followed by another festival, *Shemini Atzeret*, the Eighth day of Assembly, so that in practice, it is an eight- (or nine-) day festival. The first day (or first two days) is a festival. There are then six (or five) days of *Ḥol haMoed*, festive weekdays, and finally one (or two) festival days. *Sukkot* begins on the 15th of *Tishri*, so it is exactly six months after *Pesaḥ* according to the Jewish calendar.

The major feature of the festival in the home is the *sukkah* itself. The word *sukkah* means a hut or booth – hence the English name of the festival, the feast of tabernacles – and Jews are commanded to leave their houses for the duration of the festival and live in a temporary dwelling. This commemorates both the temporary dwellings used by the Israelites in their desert wanderings and the little huts built by farmers by their fields so they could spend every minute of the day working on the harvest. Spiritually it is a reminder of the temporary nature of material possessions, of bricks and mortar, and reinforces the belief that humanity is dependent on God's protection. The *sukkah* is built in the garden or on a balcony that is open to the sky. Most synagogues and communal institutions also build one so that those who have no garden or cannot build their own *sukkah* can use it for at least part of the festival. The sides of the *sukkah* can be built from anything – old fencing, canvas, old doors – but the roof has to be made from natural plants in their natural state, for instance, evergreen cuttings, palm branches, rushes and so on. This covering, known as the *s'khakh,* has to be thick enough to give much more shade than sun but should allow a few glimpses of the sky as well. The walls are then decorated – the children's favourite job – and the *sukkah* is ready for use. Traditionally, one should live and sleep in it and many people who live in Israel actually do, but in more northern climates it is too cold at night in October, so only the minimum requirement, that one should eat in the *sukkah,* is fulfilled. All the festival meals, including the candle lighting and the *Ķiddush,* will take place in the *sukkah* (so long as it is not raining) and most families will make an effort to fulfil the *mitzvah* of hospitality over the festival, to enable those without a *sukkah* to eat in one.

The other objects required for the festival are the *lulav* and the *etrog.* Leviticus 23: 40 commands the Jews to take four species of plants (hence the other name by which the *lulav* and *etrog* are known, *Arba'ah Minim* or the four species) to rejoice before the Lord. The four plants are the *lulav* (palm branch), three branches of *hadas* (myrtle), two branches of *aravah* (willow) and 'the fruit of goodly trees', traditionally interpreted as the *etrog* (citron). The branches are put together in a special holder so they can be held together in one hand and the *etrog* in the other. They are taken up, a blessing is recited over them, and they are waved each day during the festival. They are also used for certain parts of the synagogue celebration which are described in the section on community worship. Some of the distinctive features of the concluding festival days of *Sukkot, Shemini Atzeret* and *Shimḥat Torah,* are also considered in that section.

Yamin Noraim

The other major grouping of festivals is the New Year festivals, also known as the *Yamin Noraim* or Days of Awe. The Jewish year has two axes around which it revolves, the month of *Nisan* which is referred to in *Torah* as the first month, with its festival of *Pesaḥ* (Exodus 12: 2), and the month of *Tishri,* with the festivals of *Rosh haShanah,* the New Year, *Yom Kippur,* the Day of Atonement, and

Sukkot. In the *Torah, Rosh haShanah* is simply referred to as a day of memorial and as a day of trumpet-blowing and there is no reference to it as a New Year festival. At some later time, however, it came to have that significance and is regarded as the 'birthday of the world', the day on which creation began. As the Jews count the years from the creation of the world, the 1st of *Tishri* is regarded as the New Year for the reckoning of years and the 1st of *Nisan* as the New Year for the reckoning of the months and the festivals. The 1st of *Tishri* is also the beginning of the 10-day period which leads up to the Day of Atonement, *Yom Kippur,* so it is also the beginning of a time of reflection and soul-searching. In fact, because of the solemn nature of *Yom Kippur,* the whole of the month of *Ellul* (the month before *Tishri*) is set aside for repentance and spiritual renewal. This again can be seen as a mirror image of the physical cleansing and renewal that precedes the festival of *Pesaḥ,* six months previously.

Rosh haShanah is celebrated on the 1st and 2nd of *Tishri* both in Israel and outside it, because it was impossible to tell in advance whether the new moon would come on the 30th or the 31st day of the month before. The custom of a two-day celebration is maintained although it is not now strictly necessary as the calendar is fixed through calculation rather than observation. Most of the observances of *Rosh haShanah* are connected with the synagogue rather than the home, except certain customs of festival food. As with all festivals, candles are lit to usher in the day and *Ķiddush* is made over wine and a special meal is eaten. On *Rosh haShanah,* because it marks the beginning of a new year which, it is hoped, will be a good and prosperous one, apples dipped in honey are eaten with the prayer that God will make the new year a good and sweet one. The *Ḥallah* is usually round rather than plaited, to symbolise the never-ending cycle of the years, and many families eat other sweet foods such as carrots and honey sweetmeats. Most people also buy new clothes for the festival.

The Ten Days of Repentance, which *Rosh haShanah* initiates and which culminate in *Yom Kippur,* are used by most Jews for a spiritual stock-taking and for the process known as *teshuvah,* repentance. *Teshuvah* has four stages: recognising and regretting the ways in which one has erred; making recompense where possible – in the case of sins committed against other human beings, this requires actually asking them for forgiveness; acknowledging repentance to God; and finally, not committing the sin again should the opportunity arise. Because these stages cannot all take place on the one day, preparation for *Yom Kippur* must be made throughout the Ten Days. One can – and should – make *teshuvah* at any time, but this special time of year ensures that it is done at least at this season.

Ḥanukkah and Purim

Ḥanukkah and *Purim* are both minor festivals instituted after the time of the giving of the *Torah* and therefore involve no restriction on the kind of work that may be done.. They both commemorate God's help of the Jewish people at two particular moments of crisis.

Ḥanukkah, which means dedication, is the festival which marks the rededication of the Second Temple by the Maccabees after it had been desecrated by the Syrians. The Books of the Maccabees, which are not actually part of the canon of the Hebrew Bible, contain an account of the campaign of resistance fought from 167 to 165 B.C.E. by Judah the Maccabee and his brothers which eventually resulted in the recapture of Jerusalem. The festival is celebrated from the 25th of *Kislev* to the 2nd of *Tevet* because the re-dedication ceremonies lasted for eight days. The main element of its celebration is the lighting of *Ḥanukkah* lights, a practice we first find mentioned in the *Talmud*. The story is that the Maccabees only found one little jar of oil with the high priest's seal on it that was fit for use to light the Temple *menorah*, the seven-branched candlestick, but by a miracle, the little jar lasted for eight whole days. As a reminder of this, one more light is lit each day on the *ḥanukkiah*, the nine-branched candelabrum used for the festival, until on the eighth day, there are eight candles burning. The ninth candle is known as the 'servant' candle and is used to light the others because the *Ḥanukkah* lights themselves are only to be looked at, not used in any way. Either wax candles or oil lights are customarily used for the *ḥanukkiah*. The candles are lit each evening after nightfall and are usually placed in the window so that passers-by can see them and be made aware of the help God gave to the Jews in enabling them to defeat the Syrians. Most families also give little gifts to their children during the festival and play traditional games with a *dreidel*, the Yiddish word for a spinning top.

Purim celebrates the events recorded in the biblical book of Esther, the near-disaster averted in the 5th century B.C.E. through the moral courage of Queen Esther and her cousin Mordechai. In Esther 9: 22, the form the festival was to take is specified. There should be feasting and joy, gifts should be sent to friends and to the poor. The book of Esther is therefore read evening and morning in the synagogue. This is usually a riotous occasion because traditionally one should make a noise on hearing the name of the villain of the story, Haman, so the reading is accompanied by hooters, rattles, stamping and hissing. Special meals or parties are held. Gifts of food are sent to friends, particularly the little pastries known as *Haman-taschen*, Haman's pockets, or *oznei Haman,* Haman's ears. Contributions are also made to charity. The day is also taken as an opportunity for children to dress up as the characters of the *Purim* story and for Jewish schools to put on plays.

The emphasis of the day is mostly on enjoyment and having a good time, but the commandment to make gifts to friends and to the poor is a reminder of an appropriate way to express the joy and relief at this particular redemption of the Jewish people.

Fasts

During the Jewish year there is a series of four fasts, which are all connected in some way with the loss and destruction of the First and Second Temples in 586 B.C.E. and 70 C.E. Most of them are daytime fasts, that is, the fast is from dawn to evening only; and commemorate events such as the breaching of the wall of Jerusalem or the assassination of the last Jewish governor of the city at the time of the Babylonian destruction of the First Temple. The most significant of these fasts falls on the 9th day of the month of *Av*, roughly corresponding to August. *Tisha b'Av* marks the day on which both the First and the Second Temples were destroyed – and, coincidentally, the day of various other misfortunes that have befallen the Jewish people, such as the failure of the Bar Kokhba revolt in 135 C.E. and the expulsion from Spain in 1492. The fast is a full 25-hour one, from sunset to sunset, and it is a day of penitence and mourning. The curtain covering the ark in the synagogue is taken down, to symbolise the destruction of the Temple. People sit on low stools as they do when mourning a death and the book of Lamentations is read in the evening.

Other fasts include the fast of Esther that precedes the festival of *Purim* and the fast of the Firstborn which precedes *Pesaḥ*. The primary emphasis of all of these fasts is penitence and awareness of the consequences of sin. On the whole, they are more widely observed by the Orthodox community than by the Reform and

Liberal because the latter have tended not to emphasise the significance of the Temple in Judaism.

Community life

The centre of Jewish life is the home but each family also regards itself as part of the wider Jewish community. They will usually feel allegiance to the community, in the sense of the entire Jewish people; to the community of the town in which they live; and also to the particular community based in the synagogue which they most regularly attend. The Jewish home depends on the support of a community infra-structure, providing synagogues, educational and welfare facilities, cemeteries, shops supplying *kasher* food and a social network. Wherever possible, therefore, Jews will live in places where there is already a Jewish community or will endeavour to establish one in places where there is none or where they feel their needs are not met by the existing community.

The obvious focus for many of the community activities is the synagogue. There is no very precise indication of when the synagogue as an institution was first established, but one likely period seems to be during the Babylonian Exile after the destruction of the First Temple. There is definite evidence that it was already in existence before the destruction of the Second Temple. It is not, however, considered a holy place or a consecrated building nor is it a substitute for or replacement of the Temple. Its first major function was as a house of study, where Jews could meet together and engage in one of the prime expressions of their religious life, the study and learning of *Torah*. Only later did it become the main focus of Jewish public life and the centre for public worship which it is today. Most synagogue buildings, whether purpose-built or adapted, reflect the many functions which they serve and contain not only the room used for prayer but also a hall for community events, classrooms or rooms set aside for group study, rooms for committee meetings and so on. There are three terms used in Hebrew to cover the different functions of the synagogue. It is a *Bet Tefillah*, a house of prayer; a *Bet Midrash*, a house of study; and a *Bet Knesset*, a house of meeting (from which the English, originally Greek, word synagogue comes – it means 'to gather together'). These three categories are the easiest means by which the various activities of the community can be examined.

Bet Tefillah

As we have seen, prayer plays a large part in the daily life of the Jew and every Jew is obliged to pray each day, whether alone or with a community. However, where it is possible to pray with a quorate community, it is preferable to do so. The 'community' in this case is defined as a group of more than 10 men, whether in a synagogue building or in an *ad hoc* group convened for the purposes of one of the three daily prayer services. Most Progressive Jews have abandoned the requirement of a minimum of 10 and recite all parts of the service, regardless of the numbers present; and those who do require a *minyan* often count men and women together. Orthodox Jews will not accept a 'mixed' *minyan* but some, particularly in America, now question whether a group of 10 women cannot constitute a community. Women-only prayer communities are therefore beginning to be established there. Other Orthodox authorities maintain that women cannot form a community because their sphere is primarily private rather than public, so that a group of 10 women remains a group of 10 individuals. Certain parts of the service, particularly the call to prayer, the *Ḳedusha* or sanctification of God, which forms part of the '*Amidah,* and the *Ḳaddish*, the prayer which marks the conclusion of sections of the service and is also recited by mourners, can only be included in community prayer, not in individual prayer. The reading from the *Torah* as part of the service also only occurs in community prayer.

The prayer hall will generally contain an ark or cupboard (the *Aron haḲodesh*) set in the wall that faces towards Jerusalem, a *bimah,* a central platform from which the *Torah* will be read, and seats for the worshippers. In some synagogues there will also be a separate reading desk in front of or beside the ark where the leader of the prayers will stand; in others he or she will stand on the *bimah*. The seating arrangements will reflect the type of congregation that the synagogue serves. An Orthodox synagogue will have separate seating for men and women either with a gallery or with a section at the back or sides of the hall where the women will sit. In Progressive synagogues, everyone sits together and the *bimah* is at the front rather than in the middle so that the rabbi faces the congregation. Ashkenazi synagogues generally have all the worshippers sitting facing in the same direction whereas Sefardi ones have the seats all around the walls of the room so that the worshippers face the *bimah* and have to turn for those parts of the service where it is customary to face Jerusalem.

Most synagogues have a number of people who act as synagogue personnel, whether paid or unpaid. The title *rabbi* actually means teacher and one of the rabbi's main functions, particularly in Orthodox congregations, is still to act as a teacher of *Torah*. The rabbi is expected to have sufficient expertise in this area to be able to advise synagogue members on matters of *Halakhah*, Originally, rabbis were not paid officials of the synagogue and had some other occupation by which they earned their bread. It was only in the late mediaeval period that the phenomenon of the full-time, professional rabbi arose and it did not become common until much later. The community rabbi now has a very complex role to fill, particularly in smaller congregations. He is expected to provide spiritual inspiration through his sermons and personal example. He exercises some pastoral functions, visiting the sick or bereaved, counselling congregants with problems, and he is also expected to teach. He is not, however, a priest and has no sacramental role to play. Because of the public nature of the rabbi's role, Orthodox communities accept only male rabbis. Progressive Jews train both men and women as rabbis.

The *hazzan*, or cantor, has a more visible role in the Orthodox synagogue service because he is expected to lead the prayers throughout most of the service, whereas the rabbi may well only give a sermon and otherwise participates in the service as an ordinary member of the congregation. The custom of having someone to lead the prayers arose in the early days of the synagogue when many Jews used Aramaic as a vernacular and were not so fluent in Hebrew and were also unsure of the order of the prayers. The *sheliah tzibbur*, or representative of the congregation, would recite the prayers, particularly the 'Amidah, on behalf of the whole congregation who, by responding *Amen* to each blessing, would thereby fulfil their own prayer obligation. Even after the advent of a standardised service and, more particularly, of printing and literacy so that all members of the congregation could have and read their own prayer book, the custom was retained. The *hazzan* leads the service in the initial stages of psalms and praises by reciting the first and last lines of each psalm so that the congregation keeps more or less together and then recites the call to prayer, the *Shema* and its blessings. He repeats the 'Amidah after the congregation has said it as individuals and will probably chant the *Torah* reading according to the special cantillation. In some synagogues, there is no professional *hazzan*. The services are led by any member of the congregation who is sufficiently well versed in the *Nusah*, the traditional melodies used for chanting the service, to act as the *sheliah tzibbur*. Fewer Progressive synagogues appoint a *hazzan*, partly because more of the service is read, whereas virtually everything in the Orthodox synagogue is sung or chanted. Progressive congregations usually recite the *Amidah* in unison rather than repeating it. In such synagogues, the rabbi will probably play a more prominent role in leading the service.

The third main functionary of the synagogue is the *shammas* or beadle, whose job it is to keep the services running smoothly, for instance by making sure that everyone has a *Siddur*, a *tallit* if they need one, and that the *Torah* scrolls are rolled to the correct point for that week and so on. In most synagogues nowadays, the *shammas* is an honorary post rather than a professional one.

Shabbat and festivals in the synagogue

The main centre for the celebration of nearly all festivals is, as we have seen, the home. All the festivals are, however, also marked by special features of the synagogue service and many Jews who are unable to go to the synagogue for community prayers on weekdays will make an effort to attend on *Shabbat* and festivals.

Shabbat

The joy of celebrating *Shabbat* and the feelings of rest and relief from workday pressures mean that the Sabbath synagogue services are generally longer and more ceremonious. There is more time for the prayers to be sung to elaborate tunes and for the worshippers to feel the strength of community. This is particularly marked in the first part of the *Shabbat* evening service which is known as *Kabbalat Shabbat*, welcoming the Sabbath. Psalms 95–99 and 29 are chanted and a hymn, *Lekhah Dodi*, is sung to greet the Sabbath queen. This custom originated among the Jewish mystics of 16th century Safed, in Israel, and soon became accepted as a feature of the Sabbath services by virtually every Jewish community. Many communities also have the custom of chanting the whole of the Song of Songs at the beginning of the Sabbath evening service, understanding the text to refer allegorically to the love of Israel for the Sabbath.

The most obvious element of community prayer on *Shabbat* is the public reading of the *Torah* portion for that week. After the recitation of the morning 'Amidah, the *Aron haKodesh* is opened and the scrolls of the *Torah* are taken out and processed around the synagogue to the *bimah*. The scrolls are always treated with respect because of the words they contain and the whole congregation will therefore stand while the scrolls are being carried. The portion for that week will then be chanted and seven members of the congregation will be called up to recite the blessings before and after each section of the reading. This is known as an 'Aliyah, literally 'a going up' and is considered an honour. After the *Torah* has been read, a section of the prophetical books that is appropriate to the *Torah* reading will be chanted as the *Haftarah*, and the *Torah* scrolls are then processed back to the ark while a psalm is sung. The first part of the *Torah* portion for the next week will also be read at the afternoon service (*Minhah*). In many communities, there will be study sessions organised at the synagogue on *Shabbat* afternoons, and sometimes community celebrations such as the 'Oneg Shabbat, literally 'the delight of the Sabbath', with songs, discussion and perhaps a community meal; or the *Melaveh Malka*, 'escorting the queen', which takes place after the Sabbath has ended and the Sabbath queen is about to depart.

Pilgrim festivals

All festival services share certain characteristics and there are also distinctive features for each festival. As on the Sabbath, for the festival 'Amidah the middle 13 blessings are omitted and are replaced with a single blessing referring to the festival. On a festival, the *Hallel* is recited after the 'Amidah and before the *Torah* service. This is the name given to Psalms 113–118 which are psalms of praise: *Halleluyah* means 'praise the Lord' in Hebrew. Again, as on the Sabbath, an appropriate *Torah* portion and a *Haftarah* are read and an additional 'Amidah, the *Musaf*, is recited to commemorate the additional sacrifice offered on those days in the Temple. On a festival, the descendants of the Temple priests, the *kohanim*, go up to stand in front of the ark as the final blessing of the *Musaf* 'Amidah is recited and bless the congregation with the words of the Priestly Blessing (Numbers 6: 24–26). In the Temple, this was done every day from a special platform or *dukhan*, but in Ashkenazi communities outside Israel, is now only done on festivals. The Memorial Prayer, or *Yizkor*, is also recited on the last day of each of the pilgrim festivals.

The synagogue services for *Pesah* follow this basic pattern. The most notable addition is the prayer for dew, recited on the first day. This reflects the agricultural needs of the land of Israel at the beginning of the summer season and is recited in all communities, whether they are in the Diaspora or actually within Israel.

On *Shavuot*, many synagogues will organise a *Tikkun leil Shavuot*, an all-night study session during which material taken from all the sections of the *Torah* will be studied. This symbolises the eagerness to receive the words of *Torah* at the revelation on Mount Sinai which *Shavuot* celebrates. The Revelation is also reflected in the *Torah* reading for the first day of the festival, which includes the Ten Commandments (Exodus 19: 1–20: 26). Before the reading, hymns of love for the *Torah*, called *Akdamut*, are recited. These were composed in the 11th century in Aramaic and reflect the loyalty and love of the Jewish people for the word of God.

On *Sukkot*, there are several features which distinguish the liturgy of this festival from all others. The four species, the *Arba'ah Minim*, are brought into the synagogue on each day of the festival, except Shabbat, from the first day until *Hoshana Rabbah*, the seventh day of the festival. They are taken up, with the appropriate blessing, before the *Hallel* psalms are recited and are waved to the front, the right, behind, to the left and up and down as the first verses of Psalm 118 are chanted. This symbolises God's power over all the universe. The *Arba'ah Minim* are also carried during the *Hoshanot* when after the *Musaf* service, a *Torah* scroll is taken from the ark and is carried around the synagogue while the *Hoshana* prayer is sung. This is a hymn with the refrain *Hosha'na* – save us, of which there is a different version for each day of the festival. On *Hoshana Rabbah*, the processional is more elaborate and reflects the solemn mood of the Ten Days of Repentance and of *Yom Kippur* which precede the festival of *Sukkot*.

Shemini Atzeret, the festival which concludes *Sukkot*, is marked by the *Tefilat Geshem*, the prayer for rain. Again, as with the prayer for dew on *Pesah*, this reflects the agricultural needs of the land of Israel but has always been recited in Diaspora communities as well.

In Israel, the observance of *Shemini Atzeret* is combined with *Simhat Torah* but in the Diaspora, where the festival is celebrated for two days, they are celebrated separately. *Simhat Torah* means the Rejoicing of *Torah* and marks its never-ending cycle. The five books of Moses are read through in their entirety each year in the synagogue and on *Simhat Torah,* the cycle ends with the reading of the last verses of Deuteronomy and immediately begins again with the first verses of Genesis. In order to celebrate this event, there is uninhibited rejoicing, singing and dancing. At both the evening and the morning services, seven circuits or *Hakkafot* are made, when all of the *Torah* scrolls belonging to the community will be taken from the ark and processed around the synagogue and the members of the congregation take it in turns to dance with the scrolls. At the morning service, everybody will then be called up for an *'Aliyah,* including an *'Aliyah* for all the small children together. The final two *'aliyot* are for the very last verses of Deuteronomy and the first verses of Genesis and are considered a special honour: the two who receive this honour are known as the *Hatan Torah* and the *Hatan Bereshit,* the bridegrooms of the *Torah* and of Genesis. They customarily invite the whole congregation to a large *Kiddush* once the service is over.

Yamin Noraim

Community prayer takes a much more prominent role in the celebration of the Days of Awe, and every synagogue will have a full congregation on *Rosh haShanah* and *Yom Kippur.* In the period leading up to these festivals, many synagogues organise special prayer and study sessions to give opportunities for the spiritual renewal that should take place at this time. Particularly from the Sunday before *Rosh haShanah* till *Yom Kippur,* there will be *Selihot* services at which prayers for forgiveness are recited.

The *Rosh haShanah* liturgy has three main themes: the anniversary of creation, the kingship of God and the season of repentance and judgement. The basic pattern of all festival services is followed but there are many additions which reflect these themes, so that there is an atmosphere both of joyfulness at the beginning of a new year and of solemnity at the season of judgement. The *Torah* portion, Genesis 21 and 22, tells of the binding of Isaac, reminding Jews and (God) of the readiness of their ancestors to obey God's commands. After the reading from the *Torah* and then again during the *Musaf* service, the *shofar,* the ram's horn is blown, unless *Rosh haShanah* coincides with *Shabbat.* This reflects all of the themes of *Rosh haShanah:* the kingship of God as the trumpet is blown before a king; the remem-

brance of God's relationship with the world since the time of creation; and a call to the heart of each person for repentance. The *shofar* is also the most ancient symbolism of the day. The festival is referred to in *Torah* as a day of trumpet blowing and a day of remembering and only later came to be seen as a New Year festival.

The *Selihot* services are recited each day before morning prayers for the Days of Repentance between *Rosh haShanah* and *Yom Kippur.* The intervening Sabbath, known as *Shabbat Shuvah,* the Sabbath of Repentance, is also seen as a good opportunity for sermons or discourses from the rabbi on the theme of repentance. In fact, before weekly sermons became customary, this Sabbath and *Shabbat haGadol,* the Sabbath before *Pesah,* were the only two occasions when the rabbi would give a discourse in the synagogue.

The *Yom Kippur* services are the most solemn of the whole year. There are five services rather than the usual three of weekdays and four of festivals and virtually the whole day is spent in the synagogue. The synagogue itself is dressed for the occasion – the curtain covering the ark and the mantles that cover each scroll are changed for white ones and, particularly in an Orthodox synagogue, many of the men will wear a white robe, called a *kittel,* over their normal clothes. The colour white symbolises purity and innocence.

The observance of the day requires the Jews to 'practise self-denial' (Leviticus 16: 29). In order to achieve this, they fast for 25 hours, wash only as much as necessary, do not wear leather shoes (which are seen as a symbol of luxury) and do not have sexual relations. Before the fast begins, a meal is eaten. The table is then cleared and there is a custom of laying a prayer book in each place to symbolise the fact that the only sustenance in the next 25 hours will be spiritual not physical. The festival candles are lit and the parents bless their children. The family then goes to the synagogue for the evening service. This opens with *Kol Nidrei,* a prayer asking God to absolve the Jews from all religious vows that might be taken in the course of the next year. This is supposed to have originated at a time when many Jews were not free to practise Judaism but were forced to take formal vows denying their religion. At each of the five services, confessions of sin are recited. There are several different formulations in the liturgy but the most important is the *Al–Het* ('for the sin of . . .'), a list of ethical transgressions. The confessions are generally in the plural form, so that the sinner does not feel isolated and so that the importance of communal responsiblity is recognised.

The *Torah* reading in the morning service and the *Musaf* focus on the Temple service and on the role of the High Priest on the Day of Atonement. This was the most solemn day of all in the Temple, when the High Priest went into the innermost sanctuary to make atonement for the whole people and spoke the name of God aloud in his prayers. Since the destruction of the Temple, the whole ceremony is no longer performed and reading the account of it replaces the sacrificial ritual. The *Haftarah* reading, Isaiah 57: 14–58: 14, emphasises the importance of righteous action as well as the outward show of repentance. The final service of the day is known as *Ne'ilah,* closing up, because this is the moment when the gates of heaven, which have been open all day for the prayers of repentance, begin to close. It is the climax of the day and the prayers for forgiveness and mercy reach a new level of intensity as the congregation stands before the open ark. The prayers end with a triumphant acknowledgement of the oneness and kingship of God and a joyful awareness of the acceptance of repentance. A single call on the *shofar* marks the end of the service and of the fast-day.

Bet Midrash

The importance of study in Judaism has already been discussed with reference to the personal life of the Jew. It also plays a central role in the life of the community and is one of its most vital functions.

Most Jewish communities promote learning and study at all levels and in many different ways. The majority of synagogues organise classes for the children of the community. These might be on Sundays only or on several evenings a week, after normal school hours. Such classes generally cater for children from around the age of five until the age of *Bar/Bat Mitzvah,* and prepare them for the responsibilities and privileges that they accept at that age. In most Liberal synagogues, the classes continue until the age of 16 and end with a ceremony of Confirmation which is often held on or near the festival of *Shavuot.* In towns where there is a larger Jewish population, the community may well support a day school, in which Jewish education can be integrated into the normal curriculum and continued beyond the age of *Bar/Bat Mitzvah.*

Adult education may be supported by the organisation of regular *shiurim,* study sessions, which may be based on one particular text or may look at a certain theme and study different works relating to it. Some synagogues offer more formal programmes of evening classes, with classes in Hebrew language and all aspects of Jewish history and thought. There are usually two main motivations in providing such opportunities for study. As we have seen, study is one of the main forms of spiritual expression for Jews, enabling them to participate in the process of revelation and to come closer to understanding something of what God wants from them. Study is generally not a solitary activity and the community, after the family, is the next most obvious social unit in which study can take place. Study and education are also vital for the continuity of community life and for the transmission of the values which the community represents.

Bet Knesset

The third function of the synagogue is as a focus for the social and communal aspects of community life. Most Jewish communities have a bewildering variety of committees whose work reflects many of these different aspects. Some of these are purely social, providing opportunities for particular age or interest groups to meet and mix with each other. The majority of them, however, have as their primary function some aspect of *Gemilut Hasadim.* This concept emphasises the necessity of righteous action in order to build a just society for all. The Talmudic maxim 'each member of the community of Israel is responsible for each other' finds its practical application in activities such as caring for the elderly, sick or disadvantaged, support for other Jewish communities in difficult circumstances, for instance Russian Jews, and the raising of funds for all sorts of charitable purposes. A study of the different committees in a particular community will often give a very good idea of the many facets of this aspect of Jewish spirituality.

Public life

Introduction

This fourth area in which Jews practise their religion is the one that, by its very nature, has been most affected by the history of the Jewish people. Since the Roman destruction of the last independent Jewish state in 70 C.E., Jews have generally lived as minorities in an indifferent or even hostile host society. Participation in public life has, until relatively recently, not been an option for most Jews and there is therefore little tradition of explicit political action in the name of Judaism, as there has been in other religions where a particular religious community has been an integral part of the institutional life of the state.

In countries and periods where political emancipation has been extended to Jews, however, they have generally been eager to participate fully in public life. Judaism's teachings cover every aspect of life and have a profound influence on the way in which Jews relate to the societies in which they live. In particular, the ethical values and moral teachings of Judaism will affect the stances adopted by Jews on issues facing society at large, even by those Jews who identify themselves as 'cultural' rather than 'religious' Jews. As we have seen in the section on Jewish spirituality, the imperative of justice impels Jews to fight for a just society here on earth as one of the expressions of their belief.

Jews now live in a variety of different types of society, each of which may demand different responses from the individual:

1 Open and plural societies where a variety of religions are encouraged to participate fully in the life of the state.
2 Societies dominated by one particular religion or ideology where Judaism is seen as alien or contradictory to the beliefs and values of the state.
3 The special case of Israel, the first autonomous Jewish state for 2000 years.

In every kind of society, there are different possibilities open to the individual Jew for relating to that society. It is possible to opt out and participate as little as possible, to participate as an individual within the existing structures of the host society, or to join with other Jews to make a specifically Jewish response. The possibility of conflict between the values of Judaism and of the society in which Jews live is something that has long been recognised in Jewish teaching. The Talmudic principle of Mar Samuel, that 'the law of the country is the law', means that the civil law of the host country is predominant, provided that it does not contradict the basic principles of Jewish law. On the other hand, there are statements that are more ambivalent, such as that of Rabban Gamliel: 'Be careful in your relations with those in power because they draw men close to themselves out of self-interest, appearing friendly when they wish to but abandoning them in their time of need' (Avot 2: 4) or that of Rabbi Hanina: 'Pray for the welfare of the government since if it were not for their fear of it, men would swallow each other alive' (ibid. 3: 2).

Pressure groups

The commonest way in which Jews seek to give expression to their values and stances in political life is through pressure groups which attempt to have some influence on policies and actions of the government. In most countries, there is no one political party or platform which can be identified as 'Jewish' or with which the majority of Jews living in that country will tend to be in agreement. Specifically Jewish response, where it exists, tends therefore to be on particular issues. These may be of a general nature, such as social responsibility or nuclear disarmament, or have an element of self-interest, such as race relations and discrimination, or the welfare of Jews in countries where they are a persecuted minority or the relations of the state with the land of Israel.

Even on single issues, there is no one Jewish response and any exploration of this area would need to involve a look at the range of possible responses that exist. Particular examples might include the issue of Soviet Jewry, where groups of Jews in Western countries campaign through various means to increase public awareness of the problems faced by Jews in Russia, especially the refusal of the Soviet Union to allow them the right to emigrate to Israel. Another important issue is education about the Holocaust. The aim of this is partly as an act of memorial to the millions who died and also, more importantly, to illustrate some of the attitudes which permitted the Holocaust to happen and to fight to prevent anything similar from happening again.

The state of Israel

The existence of the state of Israel has brought the whole question of how Judaism should relate to public and political life into sharp relief, both for Jews living in Israel and for those living in the Diaspora. Again, there is an enormous range of different responses so that it is only possible to indicate some of the issues involved here.

Zionism, the movement supporting the resettlement of Jews in the land of Israel, has been an integral part of Judaism since God's promise to Abraham (Genesis 13: 14–17). There have been repeated experiences of exile and return ever since that time. The present period of exile began in 70 C.E. and the hope for a return has never been abandoned. The majority of the rabbis of the *Mishnah* and *Talmud* lived at a time when the Temple and independent Jewish statehood had already ceased to exist, yet the *Mishnah* and *Talmud* speak as if they were in fact still functioning. All the commandments that could only be fulfilled in the land of Israel and in the Temple were lovingly set down, against the day when they would be restored. The liturgy makes continual reference to the restoration of the Temple and the return of the exiles. Even in the Diaspora, the celebration of the festivals maintained constant links with the land of Israel. For instance, prayers would be recited on *Pesaḥ* and *Sukkot* for dew and rain respectively to ensure the harvests in Israel, even when there was little likelihood that those reciting the prayers would ever actually benefit from those harvests. Throughout history, there have always been at least some Jews living in Israel and there have always been those who have returned, even if the return has sometimes been a trickle rather than a flood.

The modern movement of Zionism inherited all these ingredients, as well as including elements of the other nationalistic movements that grew up in the latter half of the 19th century. There are many different forms of Zionism, ranging from traditional religious Zionism which sees the establishment of a Jewish state as part of the task of the Messiah and therefore not to be accomplished by human effort, to secular Zionists who see their national identity as sufficient expression of their Jewishness and do not observe the religion at all. The most fundamental issue is whether the state should be a religious or a secular one, which also relates to the question of what Judaism is; a race, a religion or a culture. This question is examined in the section on Jewish beliefs about the people of Israel (pp. 15–17). The tensions between religious and secular values in Israeli society are often very profound. There is also the question whether Israel should be a state like any other or whether it has particular responsibilities as the only Jewish state.

For Diaspora Jews, there are other issues such as what the difference should be between their relations with the state of which they are citizens and with Israel, how far they are entitled to comment on or criticise political life in Israel when they do not actually live there, how far they should seek to influence relations between the state in which they live and Israel, and so on.

The majority of Jews living outside Israel support her, even if they have no intention of actually going to live there, although some are opposed to the existence of a Jewish state and prefer to emphasise their allegiance to their host country. The latter attitude has become markedly less common as a response to the event of the Holocaust, which provide a terrible reminder of the vulnerability of the Jews, even in those countries like Germany where they had a long history of integration into wider society. Even so, some Jews eventually questioned the right of Zionists to found a Jewish state in the Middle East, and some today question the particular ways in which Israel now deals with the Palestinians who also lay claim to her territories. Nonetheless, the establishment of the state of Israel is seen by many as one of the major miracles of the 20th century, especially as the same century has seen the wholescale destruction of a third of the Jewish people. Some even see it as 'the beginning of the redemption', because traditionally the Messianic age is to be marked by a return to the land of Israel and they believe that so momentous a happening must in some way form part of God's plan for that redemption.

All of these issues are of very great importance to the self-understanding of Jews in the world today, whether they live inside or outside Israel and whatever their attitude is towards it. They are also very often extremely sensitive issues and great care should be exercised when dealing with this topic in the context of R.E. Again, teachers are urged to consult some of the more detailed books on the subject.

Anti-Semitism

The history of the Jewish people is interwoven with the history of anti-Semitism and anti-Judaism. Both terms denote prejudice against Jews, though strictly speaking, anti-Semitism is a 19th century term which refers more particularly to the racial origins, rather than the religious beliefs, of the Jew. Anti-Judaism predates Christianity, as can for instance be seen in the book of Maccabees or in some Latin sources dating from pagan Rome. Its most tragic manifestations, however, have been in countries where the Church has dominated the state. The reasons for anti-Judaism and anti-Semitism have been endlessly discussed, without any firm conclusions being reached. Their effects, however, have generally been only too obvious. For centuries, Jews have been denied religious freedom, allowed to live only in certain areas and to practise a restricted number of trades. They have been denied political emancipation and human dignity. Although partial political emancipation began to be granted in the last century, it is really only in the latter half of the 20th century that Christian society has begun to deal with its own anti-Semitism, mostly as a response to the

Holocaust, the end result of thousands of years of denigration and suspicion of the Jews.

The Jewish community in its turn has had to deal with anti-Semitism both negatively and positively. Negative defence takes the form of monitoring anti-Semitism in its many manifestations, for instance by noting the activities of racist organisations, many of which attack Jews as well as other ethnic minorities. Some sections of the Jewish community work together with representatives of the other minorities to combat racism. Positive defence can take the form of active dialogue with other religions, discussing some of the theological issues that have led to acrimonious feelings in the past. It can also involve educating the wider community about Judaism, on the principle that fear and suspicion feed on ignorance but not on knowledge.

SCOPE AND SEQUENCE CHART

LOWER JUNIORS	UPPER JUNIORS	LOWER SECONDARY	UPPER SECONDARY
Jewish family life A Jewish home Celebrating festivals at home *Jewish community life* Places where Jews meet Worship in the synagogue Jews helping other people	*Jewish community life* Stories about the beginnings of the Jewish people Rules and celebration of *Shabbat* Symbolic food and rituals of *Pesaḥ* *Sukkot* – a festival of belonging to the Jewish community *Purim* – a festival of bravery and loyalty Celebrating Jewish New Year Three functions of a synagogue *Jewish family life* Jewish marriage ceremonies Children in Jewish families Jewish food laws *Jewish personal life* Story of Dona Gracia Story of Elie Wiesel Story of Eve Silver	*Jewish community life* Holy places Holy times Holy people *Jewish family life* Responsibilities and privileges of Jewish family life Ceremonies which mark initiation in Jewish life Jewish family facing death *Jewish personal life* Commandments of *Torah* – a basis for personal life Jewish prayer Study – a guide to Jewish personal life	*Jewish public life* Attitudes to social issues The Holocaust The state of Israel *Jewish community life* The Jewish people Jewish diversity *Jewish spirituality* Religious experience Jewish values *Jewish beliefs* Principal Jewish beliefs

A teaching scheme on Judaism for R.E. 7–16

In this section we offer an outline of important areas of study which could be explored as one aspect of a multi-faith R.E. programme in junior and secondary schools.

A teaching scheme for use with children under seven is contained in the manual *Life Themes in the Early Years*. The intention is that children should begin their religious education in schools through work related to that scheme before engaging with the work set out here.

The Scope and Sequence Chart on page 55 indicates a way in which areas of study relating to Judaism may be distributed and approached across the 7–16 age range.

Clearly no claim is made to be able to allocate precise areas or topics for each year group in primary and secondary schools. Thus the material has been arranged within four broad age bands – lower junior, upper junior, lower secondary, upper secondary. This suggests that work on, for example, 'A Jewish home' can, and perhaps should be undertaken on several different occasions with children aged between seven and nine years. All the suggested activities for this and other areas, therefore, cannot be done at any one time. Teacher selection and adaptation is essential.

Three types of material are offered for each of the age bands to help you to plan your own R.E. programme in relation to this particular world religion.

1 A diagrammatic presentation of the key features of work suggested within the age band and how it relates to subsequent work.
2 An outline of several possible areas of study which could be undertaken with the age group.

These are developed in the four pupils' books which accompany this manual. However, there is additional material in this scheme which teachers can use to expand the work available in the pupils' books.

3 A detailed unit of work on one of the suggested areas of study.

While this teaching scheme is relatively self-contained and self-explanatory, teachers wishing to use it are advised to consult the Project manual *How do I teach R.E.?* in order to deepen their understanding of this material and how it may be used in classrooms.

In *How do I teach R.E.?* we suggest two basic approaches to the teaching of R.E. – a Systems approach and a Life Themes approach. When using a Systems approach the aim is to help pupils gain an understanding of one particular system of belief and practice, e.g. Judaism. In a Life Themes approach the aim is to help pupils expand their appreciation of some aspect of human experience which prompts many people to ask ultimate questions. A number of different traditional belief responses to these experiences and questions are then explored.

It is also important to know that in *How do I teach R.E.?* we strongly advocate that a balanced R.E. programme across the 7–16 age range must include work done according to both the Systems approach and the Life Themes approach. A failure to strike this balance could well result in a distorted and inadequate understanding of religion by pupils and thus a failure of the aims of R.E. in schools.

A case is also made in *How do I teach R.E.?* for spreading these two approaches across the 7–16 curriculum, according to the following pattern:

Age band	Approach
Lower junior	major on Life Themes approach
Upper junior	major on Systems approach
Lower secondary	major on Systems approach
Upper secondary	major on Life Themes approach

Teachers of pupils in the lower junior and upper secondary years will therefore draw a small, though very important, part of their programme from the scheme about to be described. The bulk of their material should come from the scheme set out in the Life Themes manuals.

1 Lower juniors

CHILDREN

Young children develop their understanding of ideas, beliefs and values largely through contact with people, concrete examples and stories.

JUDAISM

Judaism is expressed through a wide range of observable behaviour, concrete objects, colourful rituals and interesting stories.

EXAMPLE TOPICS

Examples of outward expressions of religious life within the context of contemporary Jewish synagogues provide a rich and effective source of content for this age group.

FUTURE WORK

Work suggested in these units lays a foundation for a more direct study of Jewish beliefs and spirituality in the secondary years.

Area of study: *Jewish family life*

Young children are interested in what happens in families and they like looking at different things that people do. The emphasis in the lower junior years is on those observable things which distinguish the family as Jewish. Beliefs and spiritual insights are implied rather than given explicit treatment. The focus is on symbolic actions and objects used by Jewish families in their regular routines and on special occasions. Some of these, especially those related to the celebration of festivals, will involve happenings at the synagogue as well as within the home, though the emphasis should be on the significance of the occasion in family life.

Topic: A Jewish home
    (a) A *mezuzah* on the doorposts
    (b) A Jewish kitchen
    (c) Rules about food
    (d) Praying at home

Topic: Celebrating festivals at home
    (a) The welcome and farewell to *Shabbat*
    (b) A family *Seder* meal
    (c) Building and using a family *sukkah*
    (d) Celebrating *Ḥanukkah* with lights

The topic worked out as a sample unit of work is 'A Jewish home'.

Content overview

Being Jewish is for many people as much about cultural identity as it is about religious belief and practice. Indeed, many Jewish people who do not participate in the religious life and practice of the synagogue still ensure that their family lifestyle reflects at least some well-established Jewish traditions. Consequently, while this unit of work should focus on the main feature of an Orthodox Jewish home, care must be taken to avoid reinforcing stereotypes. Children need to be aware of the variety of practices and customs which exist among Jewish families.

Four aspects of Jewish family life are suggested for treatment in this unit. The first two refer to observable features of the house and a study of them may therefore be better suited to the younger children within this age group. Older, and more capable children can be helped to understand the slightly more abstract rules about food and the practice of regular prayer within the family.

When dealing with each of these aspects of family life, the focus should be on the observable objects and the practices associated with these Jewish traditions. Jewish beliefs, laws and historical interpretations are implicit in these outward observances and in later years pupils will be helped to study them in a more direct way.

Aims

Knowing:
1 what a *mezuzah* looks like, what it contains and where it is placed in Jewish homes
2 some details about the way in which an Orthodox Jewish kitchen is arranged and furnished
3 the word *'kasher'* and some Jewish rules about food and drink.

Understanding:
1 that each home is different
2 that the things we have and the things we do in our houses help make them our home
3 that many Jewish people like to keep some family traditions that are thousands of years old
4 that many of the things in Jewish homes help Jewish people to remember God.

Reflecting on:
1 the ways in which our homes are special to us

2 the Jewish belief that they should obey all of God's commandments.

Activities

The following activities are some examples of work which can be undertaken to achieve the aims of this particular unit across the lower junior age band. It is left to teachers' professional judgement to select, amend, add to and sequence learning activities which suit their particular situations.

- Help the pupils to make a frieze depicting a part of their homes, for instance, their bedrooms. Discuss with them the differences between the rooms (e.g. colour of curtains, carpet) and the similarities (e.g. bed, light).
- Show picture 2 from *Jews Photopack* showing part of a Jewish kitchen. Help the children to identify features which reflect Jewish practices and beliefs, e.g. two sets of crockery and cutlery, packets of *kasher* foods.
- Make a Jewish kitchen in the classroom theme corner, stocked with Jewish foods purchased from the supermarket. Help the children to look for the Jewish food sign meaning *'kasher'* on these packets. Where appropriate allow the children to taste these foods.
- Arrange the pupils into small groups and give each a copy of the book *Jews 1*. Describe examples of meat foods and milk foods and ask the groups to make lists of one or the other. Discuss with the class the kinds of food which are a mixture of meat and milk and therefore not *kasher*, e.g. chicken supreme, lasagne.
- Play a recording of the song 'Food, Glorious Food' and then give a written copy of the song to the class. Arrange the class into groups. Ask the groups to look at one verse each and separate the foods mentioned into the categories of milk and meat, and food that does not fit into either category. Help the class to produce group collages of the different foods, putting milk foods on one side and meat on another.
- (a) Ask the class to shut their eyes and be very quiet for a few minutes and think of the oldest thing they know. Classify the answers into age categories, e.g. 10, 20, 50, 100, 1000 years old. Bring in an object which is very old (50–100 years) and see if the pupils can classify it correctly using the above categories.
  (b) Show the class some Jewish artefacts used in homes, e.g. *mezuzah, tallit, Shabbat* candles.

Ask the pupils to guess how long Jewish people have been using such things in their homes.

- Display a large card with the word 'Tradition' on it. Brainstorm with the pupils what this word means. Ask the class to list some things they do in their families that are traditions, e.g. eating together, playing certain games. The pupils may then write a descriptive passage of their favourite family traditions. These could be illustrated and mounted on card for display.
- Play the song 'Tradition' from *Fiddler on the Roof*. Discuss what he is singing about and talk about how and why Jews continue to keep these traditions in relation to the home.
- Take a *mezuzah* into the class and allow the pupils to see, touch and handle it. Draw attention to the symbols and letters depicted on the outer case and explain their meaning. Help the children to print these words and symbols on cards shaped like a *mezuzah*. These could be pinned to doorposts in the classroom.
- Divide the class into small groups and give to each group a copy of the book *Jews 1*. Help the children to find the section on the use of a *mezuzah* in Jewish homes. Explain the words 'Torah' and 'Shema'. Help the children to print out the words of the *Shema* on card or on small pieces of paper to be rolled up into a model of a *mezuzah*.
- Invite a male member of the Jewish community into the classroom to show the pupils how he prepares himself for morning prayer at home. Ask the guest to show the pupils the Jewish prayer book and to read a part of the morning prayer.
- Display a number of artefacts used by Jewish men and boys during prayer, e.g. *yarmulka*, *tallit* and *tefillin*. Using information given in this book, explain to the children the use and significance of each item. If there are any Jewish boys in the class encourage them to demonstrate how each item is worn. Decorative cards bearing the name of each item could be used to make a Jewish prayer display.

Area of study: *Jewish community life*

Judaism is one of the world's religions which does not depend for its survival on the practice of the believing community coming together for public worship and profession of faith. Judaism is essentially practised and expressed, and therefore preserved, through the life of Jewish families in their homes. Nevertheless, there are important roles for the religious observances which take place in synagogues.

Many children in the lower junior years gradually become aware of the fact that people live in different community groups, which are larger than their immediate families. For many children the school itself may be the first direct experience of this. Attending a synagogue or other religious community (e.g. church, temple, mosque, gurdwara) may also be a part of some children's experience. Certainly most of these children will be capable of understanding this feature of human behaviour. A study of the buildings in which Jews meet, linked to an expanding knowledge of the significant activities which go on there, can provide a solid base on which further understanding of Jewish community life and worship can develop in later years.

Topic: Places where Jews meet
(a) The synagogue as a place for meeting, study and prayer
(b) Synagogue furniture and its use

Topic: Worship in the synagogue
(a) *Shabbat* at the synagogue
(b) The *Torah* scrolls in the synagogue
(c) Using the Hebrew language for worship

Topic: Jews helping other people
(a) Obeying the command to love other people
(b) Jewish caring agencies

The topic worked out as a sample unit of work is 'Worship in the synagogue'.

Topic:	Worship in the synagogue

Content overview

Pupils in the lower junior classes should be familiar with some of the different buildings which are found in their own locality. Shops, the library, a factory, houses, public houses and churches are some examples.

In many areas throughout Britain there will not be a synagogue among this variety of local buildings. Pupils in these areas who belong to Jewish families and others who have had some R.E. in infant classes using the Westhill Project early years material will, of course, be familiar with the word 'synagogue' and have formed some visual images of such a building.

The basic intention of this unit is to broaden each child's understanding of the purposes of places of worship, with a particular focus on the Jewish synagogue.

Attention should be drawn to the interior design and furnishings of both an Orthodox and a Progressive synagogue. The different participatory roles played by members of each type of community should also be examined.

In later work, pupils can build on their understanding of these observable features to gain deeper insights into Jewish worship and spirituality.

Aims

Knowing:
1 the names of some important features of synagogues, e.g. ark, *Torah* scrolls, *bimah*
2 the terms *Shabbat, Kiddush, rabbi* and *ḥazzan* and what they refer to
3 what the Hebrew language looks and perhaps sounds like.

Understanding:
1 some of the observable differences between Orthodox and Progressive Jewish worship
2 some of the reasons why the Hebrew language is so important to Jews
3 that having a place to call one's own is important to most people.

Reflecting on:
1 the idea of keeping one day a week for rest and worship
2 the value of belonging to a large community.

Activities

The following activities are some examples of work which can be undertaken to achieve the aims of this particular unit across the lower junior age range. It is left to teachers' professional judgement to select, amend, add to and sequence learning activities which suit their particular situations.

- Arrange the class in small groups and give a copy of the book *Jews 1* to each group. Help them to find the story of the visit to a synagogue. After reading the story, help them to learn the meaning of such words as *Torah, bimah,* ark, rabbi and *ḥazzan.*
- Help the children to find the section on places where Jews meet in the book *Jews 1.* Discuss the physical differences between Orthodox synagogues and Progressive synagogues.
- Provide sufficient materials for the pupils to make models or draw ground plans of a synagogue. Encourage them to cut out paper to represent the main features of the synagogue furniture, e.g. ark, *bimah,* seating. Discuss the likely variations of arrangements and use between Orthodox and Progressive synagogues.
- Rearrange the classroom furniture to resemble the inside of a synagogue. Encourage the children to rearrange the items to represent (a) an Orthodox synagogue (b) a Progressive synagogue and (c) their own preference. Discuss the different arrangements and what the pupils felt about each.
- Show to the class picture 4 in *Jews Photopack* showing the synagogue as a 'house of prayer'. Using the information printed on the back of the photograph, discuss with the class the various features of the building and their uses during worship on *Shabbat.*
- Display the word *'Shabbat'* and help the children to pronounce and spell it. Explain that it is the name of the weekly holy day for Jews. Describe some of the ways in which Orthodox Jews keep this day special and different from other days of the week.
- Take the class on a visit to a synagogue. Arrange for the rabbi or another member of the Jewish community to show the children the various features of the building and to explain how they are used during the *Shabbat* worship.
- Discuss with the class some of the reasons why the *Torah* scrolls are put on the *bimah* for reading during worship: respect, easy to see and hear.
- Play a recording of the *Torah* being read in the *Shabbat* service and show the class some

Hebrew writing and its translation. Ask the pupils to read in the book *Jews 1* about the ark and *Torah* scrolls. Help the children to copy the Hebrew writing in *Jews 1* without any mistakes, writing from right to left.

- Help the pupils to design decorative scroll covers using card or coloured paper. Mount the designs on a wall or make a corridor display.
- Help the class to make models of a scroll using such articles as dollypegs, sweet tubes, velvet and felt remnants.
- Arrange the class into groups and give each group a different feature of the synagogue to draw/paint. Display these in collage form, with the word 'synagogue' in English and Hebrew as titles.
- Bring to the classroom biscuits and blackcurrant squash. Give each pupil a biscuit and drink. Tell them they can have a break and let them eat, drink and talk. Ask the pupils if they enjoyed this break and remind them about the story in *Jews 1* about Kiddush. Discuss with the class whether they think it is important to have a special time to talk with friends and family, e.g. playtime, family meals, and why they enjoy these times.

2 Upper juniors

CHILDREN

Upper primary children may be less egocentric than infants and lower junior pupils and therefore ready to consider the lifestyles and values of people different from themselves. Continued study of concrete examples of Jewish home and synagogue life is also important.

JUDAISM

Judaism is expressed through individual life-styles, and examples of this can now be used as topics along with examples from family and synagogue contexts.

EXAMPLE TOPICS

Each of the areas of study suggested can be used to introduce children in a more direct way to Jewish literature, and especially to parts of the *Torah* and other traditional stories which play formative roles in Jewish religious life.

FUTURE WORK

Work done towards the top end of this age band should relate to programmes offered in the secondary schools to which the pupils are likely to go. Liaison with these schools is highly desirable.

Area of study: *Jewish community life*

Jewish identity, in both a cultural and religious sense, has been established and developed over a period of many thousands of years. It has been maintained by people living in many different countries and in a wide range of cultural, social and political contexts. It is clearly one of the smallest of the world's religious communities, but is perhaps one of the best known. The resilience of the Jewish way of life, often in the face of intense and even violent opposition, is at once impressive and puzzling. However, two things are clear. First, the nature and quality of that identity is based on the ancient stories and laws of the Jewish scriptures, particularly the *Torah*. Secondly, the presentation and transmission of that identity is through the many regular celebrations around which a Jewish lifestyle revolves. It is this identity and the processes through which it is preserved and renewed which bind all Jews together in an international and multicultural community.

The main collective aim of all the units of work suggested within this area of study is to give older primary children broader and deeper understanding of these stories, laws and celebrations.

Topic: Stories about the beginnings of the Jewish people
    (a) God makes the world
    (b) God's covenant with the Jews
    (c) God gives the land to the Jewish people

Topic: The rules and celebration of *Shabbat*
    (a) The welcome to *Shabbat*
    (b) The *Shabbat* lifestyle
    (c) The farewell to *Shabbat*

Topic: The symbolic food and rituals of *Pesaḥ*
    (a) The food on the *Seder* plate
    (b) The ritual of the *Seder*

Topic: *Sukkot* – a festival of belonging to the Jewish community
    (a) The *sukkah*, the *etrog* and the *lulav*
    (b) Celebrating *Simḥat Torah* in the synagogue

Topic: *Purim* – a celebration of bravery and loyalty
    (a) The story of Queen Esther
    (b) *Purim* celebrations at the synagogue

Topic: Celebrating the Jewish New Year
    (a) Remembering the day the world began
    (b) Receiving the forgiveness of God

Topic: The three functions of a synagogue
    (a) The house of prayer
    (b) The house of meeting
    (c) The house of study

The topic worked out as a sample unit of work is 'Stories about the beginnings of the Jewish people'.

Topic	Stories about the beginnings of the Jewish people

Content overview
Stories are important to most religious communities. This is particularly so in regard to those stories which are told over and over again within the regular worshipping activities and rituals of the believing community.

Three stories are suggested for study in this unit. While the connections between these stories and present day Jewish celebrations will be highlighted in subsequent units, the emphasis here is on the stories themselves and the ideas they convey about God and God's relation to the Jewish people.

The stories of Abraham and Moses are very long and should not be told in their entirety at this stage. The emphasis in the Abraham story is on the covenant or promise between God and Abraham and Sarah and the threat to that in the command to sacrifice Isaac. The emphasis in the Moses story is on the giving of the commandments during the long journey from Egypt to the Promised Land. The equally important parts of the story which tell of the Passover and the escape of the slaves from Egypt are told in *Jews 1* in this series and are recommended for study by younger children.

Aims
Knowing:
1 in a broad outline, the Jewish stories of creation, Abraham and Moses

2 the word 'covenant' and what it means to Jewish people
3 the Ten Commandments.

Understanding:
1 the importance of ancient stories in religious traditions
2 different ways of thinking about the origins of the world
3 the reasons why many people think that obedience to God is more important than anything else.

Reflecting on:
1 the belief that God chooses people for special roles and tasks
2 the belief that the Ten Commandments are God's rules for all people.

Activities
The following activities are some examples of work which can be undertaken to achieve the aims of this particular unit across the upper junior age group. It is left to teachers' professional judgement to select, amend, add to and sequence learning activities which suit their particular situations.
● Show the children pictures of the 'world', e.g. countryside, seashore, different countries. Divide the class into small groups and give one picture to each group. Help the children to list what they like or dislike about their particular picture.

- Ask the children how they would go about 'creating' or laying out their own ideal world, town or garden. Using their initial ideas, help them to express these through various forms of creative work, e.g. painting, collage, sewing, writing.
- Read or ask the children to read the creation poem in the book *Jews 2*. Perhaps another poem or story of creation could be read, e.g. 'Creation' by the American writer James Weldon Johnson. Ask the children working in groups to find and list the differences, if any, between the poems and stories.
- Show a video or other audio-visual presentation of the biblical creation poem or story. Discuss the artist's impressions and/or the musical accompaniment to the story. Help the children to create their own imaginative ideas of the story through such media as art, music or movement.
- Discuss with the children some of the concerns about the world expressed by such groups as conservationists like Friends of the Earth. Show a series of pictures which illustrate some of the things that are happening to the natural world which prompt these things. Introduce the idea of belief in God as creator of the earth and discuss whether holding such beliefs makes any difference to the way people treat or care for the world.
- Divide the children into small groups and give each group pictures of different signs and notices which require them to take action. Ask them whether they regard the signs as orders (e.g. traffic light) or as information (e.g. 'Library'). Discuss the differences and ask the children to make two lists of commonly used signs. In one list, group those which give orders they have to obey and in the other, those which give them information.
- Provide sufficient and appropriate materials to allow the children to make some signs, either as posters or models, of what they regard as orders which they must obey.
- Distribute copies of the book *Jews 2* and help the children to read the story 'God's covenant with the Jewish people'. Explain the idea of 'covenant' or two-way promises.
- Encourage the children to share their reactions to the idea of travelling to an unknown land without any directions. Help the children to discuss in small groups how they might plan for such a journey. What would they take? How would they decide on a direction? What things should they be prepared for? (e.g. different types of terrain, weather and people).
- Show pictures or audio-visuals of the Fertile Crescent and explain, by use of maps, the exact location of the area in which the story of Abraham is set.
- Prepare a large wall frieze on which children can create various scenes from the story of Abram and Sarai.
- Help the children to re-enact scenes from the story of Abram and Sarai using various forms of drama, e.g. play reading, mime, movement.
- Display the names 'Abram' and 'Sarai' and 'Abraham' and 'Sarah'. Point out how the names were changed. Ask the children to try altering their names. Discuss the results. Encourage them to think of some reasons they might want to change their names.
- Divide the class into small groups and give each group a copy of the book *Jews 2*. Help the children to find the story of Moses leading the people through the desert towards the land they were promised. After reading the story encourage the children to talk about the things that happen in the story and about the parts they liked or disliked the most.
- Display copies of the Ten Commandments. Discuss the meaning of some of these and respond to the children's questions about these commandments. Encourage some conversation about the belief that these are God's commandments for all people.
- Help the class to prepare a set of explanations to be given to God about why some people today cannot or will not keep all of the Ten Commandments.

Area of study: *Jewish family life*

Three aspects of Jewish family life are suggested for study with upper juniors who are learning about Jews through the Systems approach as recommended in the Westhill Project teacher's manual *How do I teach R.E.?*

By this age many pupils will have some ideas about wedding ceremonies, gained either from attending one or through such other agencies as the media, books or school activities. In R.E. the concentration is on ways in which people bring quite explicit religious beliefs and practices to bear on their marriage ceremonies.

The second area of Jewish family life recommended for study with this age group focuses on ceremonies associated with the initiation of children into a Jewish way of life. Circumcision and *Bar/Bat Mitzvah* ceremonies are among the more important of these rituals.

Rules and teachings about appropriate food and drink are also important features of Jewish family life. A study of these and some of the reasons which Jews offer for keeping them may help all pupils reflect on the effect that their eating habits will have on their lifestyle, their health and perhaps on the health of the communities to which they belong.

Topic: Jewish marriage ceremonies
(a) The symbolic *huppah*
(b) Prayers, blessing and contracts

Topic: Children in Jewish families
(a) Circumcision
(b) Naming
(c) *Bar/Bat Mitzvah* ceremonies

Topic: Jewish food laws
(a) *Kasher* foods
(b) Ritual slaughter
(c) Meat and milk

The topic worked out as a sample unit of work is 'Children in Jewish families'.

Topic	Children in Jewish families

Content overview

Most children in this age group are becoming increasingly aware of the ways in which important features of their personal identity are derived from their families. They know that their racial, national and perhaps regional identity has come to them through their families. Part of the role of education, and therefore of religious education, is to help each child form positive attitudes to this heritage and to become increasingly mature in responding to its possibilities and challenges. Learning about the way in which other families value and seek to preserve and enrich their traditions can make an important educational contribution to this process of maturation.

Jewish traditions are preserved and renewed primarily through family life. Consequently, there is a strong desire among many Jews that marriage should be between Jew and Jew. 'Marrying out' is often perceived to be a very serious threat to the survival of Judaism. As one expression of this, the role of Jewish parents, especially the mothers, in nurturing each generation of children into a Jewish lifestyle is considered to be crucial for the survival of the tradition.

In the previous units of work children will have met the word 'circumcision' through the stories of Abraham and Moses. Now they can be introduced to a few of the details of this practice and to Jewish beliefs about it as an important aspect of keeping their side of the covenant believed to be made between them and God.

The practice of choosing names which also link the younger generation with the long tradition of the Jewish people can also be explored in ways which highlight the importance of preserving racial, cultural and religious identity.

The preparation for *Bar* and *Bat Mitzvah* and for the increasing responsibilities within the community required of those who have reached this stage of their life also offers appropriate areas of knowledge and understanding for children in upper junior classes.

Aims

Knowing:
1 the word 'circumcision' and some details of the ceremony carried out eight days after the birth of a baby boy
2 at what age girls and boys are recognised as being *Bat* or *Bar Mitzvah* in Jewish communities, and what responsibilities they then have.

Understanding:
1 the idea of a covenant and why Jews believe that they have a covenant with God
2 some of the reasons why Jewish people value family life and traditions so highly
3 why some people consider that personal names are important to both the individual and to a community.

Reflecting on:
1 the value of family customs and traditions
2 the possibilities and challenges of marriage between people of different race, nationality and/or religion.

Activities

The following activities are some examples of work which can be undertaken to achieve the aims of this particular unit across the upper junior age range. It is left to teachers' professional judgement to select, amend, add to and sequence learning activities which suit their particular situations.

- Look at the picture of a mother and baby in *Jews 2*, p. 48. Read to the class the sentence beside the picture: 'Anybody whose mother is Jewish is automatically a member of the Jewish community' and discuss with them what this means.
- Display the title 'I promise...'. Arrange the class into small groups and ask each group to think of some promises that they feel are important to keep. Help the pupils to write these out and display under the title 'I promise...'.
- Show the class a certificate/badge that represents a promise, e.g. Guides/Scouts; Jewish marriage certificate; product guarantee. Discuss with the pupils why these promises are important.
- Read the story of Abraham and Sarah in *Jews 2* to the class. Encourage the pupils to mime out the story as it is read a second time.
- Enable the class to perform a play along the following lines: *Parents:* 'We are going to visit Grandma this weekend.' *Children:* 'Why do we have to go?' Encourage the pupils to incorporate ideas of duty, family traditions, love. Draw the connection between this kind of scenario and circumcision.
- Ask the pupils to write and decorate their names for a display.
- Encourage the class to discuss such questions as who chose their name and why. Ask the pupils if they know whether they were named after anybody who is important to their family, and why this might be done (e.g. love, respect, tradition).

- Read the section in *Jews 2* on 'Naming' to the class. Write on the board the examples of names that are popular with many Jewish families. Ask the pupils if they have any Jewish friends and what their names are.
- Give the pupils examples of names which are found in other languages, but spelt or said in a different way, e.g. John, Johann, Jean; Anne, Anya, Anita, Anastasia.
- Encourage the pupils to make various kinds of graphs to represent the distribution of names within their class/school. Using the graphs, discuss with the class why they think some names appear more often than others.
- Arrange the pupils in groups and ask them to read the section in *Jews 2* on *Purim*. Ask the pupils why they think a Jewish family would name a daughter Esther, but not name a son Haman.
- Arrange pupils into groups to read *Jews 2* p. 50 on *Bat/Bar Mitzvah*. Ask the class why they think the word 'adult' is in quotation marks in the text. Discuss the legal definition of the term 'adult'.
- Display the current cinema film ratings (U, 12, PG, 15, 18). Encourage the class to discuss why these are set, by whom and whether they think the system is fair.
- Consider with the class at what ages different responsibilities and privileges are given (e.g. staying out late, crossing the road alone, helping with the housework, babysitting) and who makes these decisions.
- Discuss with the class how they think the children should be brought up when the parents come from different religious traditions (e.g. if the mother is Jewish and the father is Christian) and the importance this might have.

Area of study: *Jewish personal life*

Being a Jew is a very personal and individual matter. This does not mean that it is something that any person can choose to be on the basis of some private desire. Even less is it suggesting that people can decide, in a totally individualistic way, what being Jewish entails. The Jewish way of life is steeped in a very long tradition, stretching back over many thousands of years. People who have a Jewish mother are automatically considered to be Jewish and thereby become an integral part of the community. Nevertheless, it is true that all members of the Jewish community have to live out their own personal lives in their own way. Preserving one's own religious and cultural identity as a Jew is a matter of choice and commitment.

Countless numbers of Jews down through the ages have felt pressure on them to renounce this aspect of their personal identity. At times this pressure has taken excessive and violent forms. Consequently, the stories of people who have withstood such pressures are of immense value to the Jewish people.

Equally, the purposes of R.E. in helping all children to develop mature individual patterns of belief and behaviour are well served by reference to such stories of faith and perseverance. Later on, in the secondary years, pupils can be helped to look more closely at the beliefs and values which Judaism offers as a spiritual framework within which Jews seek to live their personal lives in accordance with what they believe to be the will and commandments of God.

Topic: The story of Dona Gracia
(a) Being afraid to be Jewish
(b) Standing up for her faith
(c) Helping the persecuted Jews

Topic: The story of Eve Silver
(a) Growing up in Manchester
(b) Setting up a new Jewish home

The topic worked out as a sample unit of work is 'The story of Dona Gracia'.

Topic	The story of Dona Gracia

Content overview
Children in the upper primary school are beginning to be more aware of their own personal characteristics and abilities. In consequence, they may be trying to establish or assert their own individuality. This can be linked with their interest in stories, especially stories of individuals who have achieved something worthwhile, perhaps in spite of great difficulties or opposition.

Many of these children are also developing their sense of fairness in human relationships and this particular story may help them move towards a greater understanding of the complexity and importance of this moral concept.

Anti-Semitism has been present in many countries for many centuries. It has played a significant role in shaping Jewish self-images and in formulating a particular kind of spirituality. For some Jews it results in a desire to live within a tightly knit community motivated by a tenacious will for survival and self-preservation. For others, the experiences of deep and sometimes prolonged suffering have created and sustained a sense of unity with all suffering people and a commitment to seek justice for all who are oppressed.

Perhaps something of these two qualities of spirit is expressed in the story of Dona Gracia as told in *Jews 2*.

When using this story teachers should help the children to understand the historical and personal particularities of it. This should help them in the important task of avoiding the reinforcement of stereotypes – whether of Jews or Christians. Nevertheless, the general lessons to be learnt about religious and other forms of bigotry and unjust persecution is also an important feature of the aims of this unit.

Aims
Knowing:
1 in general outline, the story of Dona Gracia

2 the word 'prejudice' and what it means.

Understanding:
1 that it is not always easy for people to declare openly their religious faith
2 that prejudice against groups of people is often based on misunderstanding and ignorance.

Reflecting on:
1 the value of racial, national and religious differences among people
2 the importance of fairness and justice in human relationships in families, school and communities.

Activities
The following activities are some examples of work which can be undertaken to achieve the aims of this particular unit across the upper junior age range. It is left to teachers' professional judgement to select, amend, add to and sequence learning activities which suit their particular situations.
- Show the class pictures of people in 14th century European dress. Encourage the pupils to depict figures on a frieze in this type of costume, perhaps representing the characters of the story.
- Play a piece of music expressing feelings of fear, anxiety, escape, (e.g. 'Night on Bear Mountain') while reading paragraphs two and three of the Dona Gracia story. Play the music again, asking the class to dramatise through movement the feelings expressed in the story and the music.
- Encourage the class to pretend to be a news team doing a half-hour news special on the life of Dona Gracia, including interviews, news reports, etc. Encourage full participation of the class with parts such as camera operators, reports, lighting engineers, producers, etc.
- Ask the class to think of a name that they might like to be called instead of their real name and discuss why. Talk about the different

reasons why Dona Gracia changed her name several times. Encourage pupils to think about and discuss how they would feel if they had to change their name to hide something about themselves.

- Ask the class to close their eyes and think of a secret about themselves, something that they would not want the whole class to know. Encourage them to think of reasons why and to imagine how they would feel if other people found out. With their eyes still closed, ask them to pretend they are Beatrice de Luna and to imagine what might happen to them if people found out their secret.
- Arrange the class into a circle, either standing or sitting very close together, facing towards the centre. Ask one pupil to walk round the outside and ask to join the circle. Instruct the class to ignore these requests and refuse entrance. Encourage the pupil to express how this feels. Repeat the exercise with different pupils taking the role of the one who asks to join the circle. Ask the pupils in the circle how they felt when refusing entrance.
- Display a sentence such as 'The people of Thickopolis can't read'. Ask the class how they might feel towards these people if they met

them and write their reactions on the board. Then display an opposite sentence, e.g. 'The people of Thickopolis can read very well'. Inform the class that the second sentence is the true one, and that they were deliberately misinformed the first time. Ask them how they feel about their original statements, now they know the truth.

- Encourage the class to produce a short drama along the following lines: a group of children are all reacting in a hostile and prejudiced manner towards a new member of the class. One person in the group shows positive support towards the newcomer and receives varying reactions from the group.
- Pin a card on each child with a descriptive word written on it, e.g. strong, gentle, brainy, fast, tall, small, practical, etc. Give different problems that the whole class must solve and ask them which people would be of most help to the whole group. For example, if a bird is hurt, who would best help – 'Gentle', to care for bird or 'Fast', to fetch help; or if the class is all accidentally locked out in the rain with only a high, small window open, who would be most useful – 'Strong', to lift up or 'Small', to climb through.

3 Lower secondary

CHILDREN

Pupils in the lower secondary school need to see clear links between what they have learned in the primary school and new work presented to them. However, progression is also essential. The acquisition of new knowledge and greater demands on their intellectual and emotional abilities are looked for.

JUDAISM

Judaism, as well as being expressed in outward behaviour, provides a set of reasons and a source of motivation for particular beliefs and actions.

EXAMPLE TOPICS

The general areas of study used in the upper junior school are retained for this group. However, new material is introduced and greater attention is paid to the reasons and motivations for Jewish behaviour.

FUTURE WORK

Work with this age group must build on previous experiences and move pupils towards further specialised, in-depth study. Success in recruiting for, say, examination groups is largely dependent on presentation of this subject at this stage.

Area of study: *Jewish community life*

To be Jewish does not necessarily involve being 'religious'. An individual's identity within the worldwide Jewish community is based on three important common factors: a shared history, the Hebrew language, and the land of Israel. Even in the centre of the local Jewish community, the synagogue, activities which are not overtly religious, such as social action and community care, are as central as corporate worship and *Torah* study.

Judaism tends not to draw a sharp distinction between secular and sacred activities. Belief in God and action in response to God's love are inseparable in Jewish thought. So, running a home for the elderly or caring for those who mourn are both activities which may be seen as 'religious' in an important sense.

At the same time the concept of 'holiness' plays a role in Jewish life. The Hebrew word for holiness, *ḵedusha*, implies separateness, distinctness. God is seen as completely 'other' and much greater than humanity can begin to understand.

Holiness in Judaism implies actions or beliefs that draw God and God's greatness into everyday life and allow people to be aware and experience God in their life.

The following topics are intended to assist lower secondary students to begin to explore the place of holy times, places and people in Jewish community life.

Topic: Holy places
  (a) Jerusalem and the Temple
  (b) The synagogue
  (c) The home

Topic: Holy times
  (a) *Shabbat*
  (b) Festivals of the *Torah*
  (c) Post-*Torah* festivals

Topic: Holy people
  (a) Priests and Levites
  (b) Rabbis
  (c) Students of the *Torah*

The topics worked out as a sample unit of work is 'Holy times'.

Topic	Holy times

Content overview
In the Jewish community certain times are set aside in which Jews are especially reminded of God and their relationship with God. In this way the holiness of God is drawn into the time of ordinary life, making those times holy.

The most important 'holy time' is *Shabbat*, the Sabbath. *Shabbat* is a day of rest, an 'island of time', given over wholly to remembering God and enjoying what God has provided. Because *Shabbat* happens every week its celebration is a focal point of Jewish life.

In preparation for *Shabbat*, all food is cooked in advance, the house is cleaned and the family bathes and puts on clean clothes to welcome in the Sabbath. Celebration of *Shabbat* begins on Friday evening with some of the family members attending synagogue service to return to a special meal at which traditional prayers, songs and foods contribute to a relaxing evening – a time 'set apart' to enjoy God's gifts and each other's company. Saturday may be spent in worship, relaxation and *Torah* study. *Shabbat* finishes with a beautiful, symbolic ceremony in the home which marks the transition from 'holy time' back to ordinary time.

The festivals of the *Torah* are other 'holy times' at which various historical events and moments important to the Jewish community and its relationship to God are celebrated. These are celebrated because God, through the *Torah*, communicated that these times should be set apart. These times include the pilgrim festivals (*Pesaḥ*, *Shavuot* and *Sukkot*) and the New Year festivals (*Rosh haShanah* and *Yom Kippur*).

Festivals such as *Purim*, *Ḥanukkah*, various fasts, rabbinic festivals and modern celebrations such as Israeli Independence Day and Holocaust Remembrance Day have not been laid down in *Torah* but are celebrated to commemorate some important aspect of Jewish life or history. They also set aside time and make it holy in their celebration.

Aims
Knowing:
1 some of the ways the Jews celebrate *Shabbat*
2 the basic differences between the Jewish calendar and the Common Era calendar
3 some of the ways Jewish festivals are celebrated.

Understanding:
1 the essence of what Jews mean by the word 'holiness'
2 some of the ways in which the celebration of festivals are important to Jewish community life
3 some of the reasons why *Shabbat* is celebrated.

Reflecting on:
1 the belief that God's holiness can enter daily life through 'holy times'
2 the concept of 'rest' and 'work' reflected in the celebration of *Shabbat*
3 the Jewish belief that the setting aside of holy times is commanded by God.

Activities
The following activities are some examples of work which can be undertaken to achieve the aims of this particular unit across the lower secondary range. It is left to teachers' professional judgement to select, amend, add to and sequence learning activities which suit their particular situations.

- Ask the class to brainstorm activities, putting them into two lists – those which are work and those which are not work. Distribute *Jews 3* to the class and ask them to read about *Shabbat*. Split the pupils into two groups. Encourage one group to list activities that Judaism defines as work and the other group to list activities which Judaism regards as not work.
- Show to the class picture 3 from *Jews Photopack* of a family enjoying a *Shabbat* meal. Using the information on the back of the photograph, describe some of the special preparations and food for the *Shabbat* celebration.

- Discuss with the class what foods they eat when celebrating special days. Encourage the pupils to think about why special foods are used in celebrations.
- Invite a member of a Jewish family to show the class how a *Shabbat* table is laid, including such items as Ḥallah, Ḳiddush cup and candles.
- Using a video or slides, show the class a family celebrating the *Shabbat* meal, and the rituals associated with the inauguration of *Shabbat*, e.g. lighting of candles, blessing the children, singing.
- Ask the pupils to design a poster depicting the differences between the Jewish calendar and the Common Era calendar.
- Distribute copies of *Jews 3* to the class. Ask them to find any themes that are common to several of the festivals, e.g. agriculture, repentance, important historical events.
- (a) Taking *Purim* as an example, help the pupils to explore the qualities of the historical figures involved that may have contributed to the continuing celebration of the festival.
  (b) Explore with the class questions such as, 'How does remembering events of the past affect the Jewish community today?' and 'Does remembering the Second World War help to prevent a Third World War?'
- Distribute copies of *Jews 3* to the class and ask them to read the section on *Ḳadosh* near the beginning of Part 1. Ask the pupils what times, places, people they consider to be special or set apart and why they feel that way about them.

Area of study: *Jewish family life*

Jewish family identity and bonds are built up to a large extent through family experiences and the shared practice which results from common belief. In this section, the three suggested topics are intended to help pupils to explore how customs and traditions help to build and strengthen family ties.

The first topic explores the nature of the parent/child relationship in Jewish family life. It is intended to bring out the responsibilities and privileges of parents and children in a Jewish family and to look at shared experiences, family prayer and family learning.

The second topic looks at how the preparation for and the ceremony of a *Bar* or *Bat Mitzvah* mark the transition from childhood to adulthood in Jewish families. The third is intended to help pupils to explore how Jewish belief and practice contribute to helping a Jewish family deal with the experience of a death in the family.

Topic: The responsibilities and privileges of Jewish family life
  (a) sharing family life experiences such as birth or a death
  (b) learning about the faith as a family
  (c) praying as a family
  (d) the relationship between parents and children

Topic: Ceremonies which mark initiation in the Jewish way of life
   (a) preparation for *Bar/Bat Mitzvah*
   (b) the ceremony of *Bar/Bat Mitzvah*
   (c) the meaning of adulthood in Judaism

Topic: The Jewish family facing death
   (a) Jewish beliefs about death
   (b) Jewish practices on the occasion of a death
   (c) Jewish mourning customs

The topic worked out as a sample scheme of work is 'The Jewish family facing death'.

Topic	The Jewish family facing death

Content overview

The traditions and customs which are carried out at the time of a death in a Jewish family highlight the inseparable relationship between belief and practice. The activities in the following sample scheme of work are designed to help the lower secondary pupil explore both family practices at the time of a death and the beliefs that inform these practices.

A belief which is central to Judaism is that God is to be remembered and praised at all times. This belief is reflected in the custom of a dying person repeating the words, 'Hear O Israel! The Lord is our God, the Lord alone.' This belief is also evident in the words of *Kaddish*, a prayer of praise to God said in the process of mourning.

The very simple coffin and shroud used for everyone, rich or poor, reflects the Jewish belief in the equality of all human beings. Respect for the dead is reflected in many practices, including the reverent way that bodies are washed and laid out by the *Ḥevra Kadisha* (the 'holy society') and the custom of burying the dead as soon as possible.

The importance of family ties and the special relationship between parents and children is reflected in mourning traditions. Most Orthodox families stay at home for a week after a death to receive friends who will call to show support and share their sorrow. The family continues to remember the deceased after that week by abstaining from celebrations for the next three weeks and by saying *Kaddish* every day, and for another 10 months if mourning a parent.

The activities are intended to help the pupils to focus on both the importance of the family and family relationships at the time of the sad occasion of death and to reinforce the idea that Judaism is a religion whose beliefs call forth action in family life.

Aims

Knowing:
1 some of the customs and traditions which surround death and burial

2 some of the practices involved in mourning a death in the family
3 the role of the *Ḥevra Kadisha*
4 the meaning of an 'ethical will'.

Understanding:
1 some aspects of the connection between Jewish beliefs about death and the customs that grow out of these beliefs
2 the importance of giving mourners a chance to express grief
3 in what sense the *Ḥevra Kadisha* is seen to be holy.

Reflecting on:
1 the role of the community in helping families to cope with death
2 the equality of all human beings which is highlighted in Jewish burial customs
3 the importance and value of life as expressed in customs practised at death.

Activities

The following activities are some examples of work which can be undertaken to achieve the aims of this particular unit across the lower secondary range. It is left to teachers' professional judgement to select, amend, add to and sequence learning activities which suit their particular situations.
- Distribute copies of *Jews 3* and ask the class to find passages in the text that explain how Jews show respect to the dead. Ask the pupils to consider how the family might be comforted and helped by knowing that the person they loved is treated with respect after death.
- Ask two pupils to read out the interview with Mrs Winnie Abrahams, an Orthodox member of the women's *Ḥevra Kadisha*. Encourage the class to discuss why the *Ḥevra Kadisha* is considered to be a 'holy' society.
- Discuss with the class the Jewish tradition of burial using only the simplest coffin and shroud, regardless of wealth and status. Ask the pupils how they feel about this, and if they feel that this might be a good general principle.

- Distribute copies of *Jews 3* and ask the pupils to read the section, 'Ethical wills'. Ask the pupils to write their own ethical wills, stating values that are important to them.
- Using picture 14 in *Jews Photopack* of a Jewish grave, ask pupils to think of the custom of remembering the dead with a gravestone. Encourage them to think about why certain things might be written on the stone (and why they are in Hebrew in the picture) and what role the placing of gravestones might play in the mourning process.

Area of study: *Jewish personal life*

What is distinctive about Jewish personal life is that it is structured within the framework of the commandments or *mitzvot* of the *Torah*. In Jewish belief the purpose of the commandments is to help the community and the individual to live out God's nature in every aspect of daily life. The commandments help to shape life and make it possible to do God's will and to remember God throughout life.

Each individual's attempt to carry out these commandments naturally results in different behaviour. However, because of the unifying force of *Torah*, personal life in Judaism has many common elements. Most Jewish people will try to use the *Torah* to try to find out about the nature of God and to form their values by which they live their life to reflect these qualities.

The commandments of the *Torah* provide the precepts for two basic types of relationship, the relationship between an individual and God and the relationship between individuals. The first type of *mitzvah*, governing the relationship between God and human beings, includes the commandments that refer to prayer, to the keeping of the Sabbath and the laws of *kashrut*. The second type, governing the relationship between human beings, primarily deals with ethical and moral matters.

The three suggested topics are designed to help pupils explore the relationship between *Torah* (and, to some extent, the prophetic books and teaching of the rabbis) and the complexities of Jewish personal life.

Topic: The commandments of *Torah* as a basis for personal life
   (a) Life as governed by the freedom to serve God
   (b) Commandments governing the relationship between God and human beings
   (c) Commandments governing the relationship between one human being and another

Topic: Jewish prayer
   (a) The *Shema* ('Hear O Israel . . .')
   (b) Morning, afternoon and evening prayer
   (c) Blessings
   (d) Spontaneous prayer

Topic: Study as a guide to Jewish personal life
   (a) The purpose of study – learning about God
   (b) Study of *Torah*, a central commandment
   (c) Study of the works of the prophets and rabbis

The topic worked out as a sample unit of work is 'Jewish prayer'.

Topic	Jewish prayer

Content overview

The commandments governing the relationship between God and humanity shape both the forms that prayer takes and the purpose of prayer in Jewish personal life. Some of the main reasons individuals may pray are to communicate with God and hear God communicate with them. The knowledge that comes from this communication may help bring God's holiness into daily life.

The times for individuals to pray are (1) at stated times (morning, afternoon, evening); (2) on various occasions (a blessing is said before various acts or events); and (3) whenever a person wishes to communicate with or praise God.

Prayer is made up of various elements, including praise and thanksgiving to God and self-examination. The self-examination aspect helps people to look at their behaviour, in some sense, in the presence of God.

Aims

Knowing:

1 the meaning of some important terms such as *mitzvah*, *Shema* and *tefillah*

2 the basic types of prayer practised by Jews – prayers said morning, afternoon and evening; blessings; spontaneous prayer

3 some of the themes that recur in Jewish prayer.

Understanding:

1 the concept of blessing and why blessings are said in Jewish daily life

2 some of the reasons Jews pray as individuals.

Reflecting on:

1 the role of prayer in shaping daily life

2 the Jewish idea that 'freedom' is essentially freedom to serve God

3 why Jews put such emphasis on praising God.

Activities

The following activities are some examples of work which can be undertaken to achieve the aims of this particular unit across the lower secondary range. It is left to teachers' professional judgement to select, amend, add to and sequence learning activities which suit their particular situations.

- Show the class picture 1 from *Jews Photopack*, and read the information concerning *tefillin*. Distribute copies of *Jews 3* and ask the pupils to read the second paragraph in the section 'Prayer' from the part on 'Jewish personal life'. Display the words *'tefillah'* (prayer) and *'tefillin'* (phylacteries). Ask the class to speculate on how these words might interrelate and explore the belief that prayer involves 'judging oneself'.

- Ask the pupils to examine the examples of prayer in the text, looking for recurring themes (i.e. praise, marking beginnings and endings, everyday actions).

- Ask the pupils to brainstorm what they might do to remind themselves of somebody they love who has moved away (e.g. keep photographs, write letters, go to certain places that they had gone with that person, etc.). Encourage the class to imagine how regular prayers and blessings throughout the day remind Jews of God.

- Divide the class into small groups. Ask them to think of some time or event in their day that they feel is important to them and worth highlighting. Encourage each group to design a poster depicting this time or event and to write an appropriate blessing on the poster.

- Show photographs 1 (daily prayer in *tallit* and *tefillin*) and 4 from *Jews Photopack* (synagogue as a place of prayer) to the class. Encourage them to explore the relationship between individual and corporate prayer and to look at the differences and similarities between these types of prayer.

- Distribute copies of *Jews 3* and ask the pupils to read the introduction to 'Jewish personal life'. Display the phrases 'Freedom to . . .' and 'Freedom from . . .' and ask the class to brainstorm how they would complete these phrases, both from a personal and from a community perspective. Ask the class to explore the Jewish belief that freedom is not only from oppression but freedom to serve God.

- Distribute copies of *Jews 3* and ask the pupils to read the section 'The Commandments (*mitzvot*)'. Ask the pupils to explore the idea that the following of God's commandments makes Jewish life 'holy'. Encourage the class to use the photographs in the text of different actions and blessings to discuss the belief that all areas of daily life can be made holy.

- Invite a male member of the Jewish community to the classroom. Ask him to show the pupils the *tallit* and *tefillin* and to talk to the class about their use and meaning in Jewish daily prayer.

- Ask the class to look at the words of the *Shema* (Deuteronomy 6: 4–9). Discuss with the pupils how this statement is used as a prayer and its unifying role in community life.

4 Upper secondary

CHILDREN

In the upper secondary school pupils should be helped to establish a comprehensive overview of several different belief systems. The units suggested here seek to contribute to this aim while at the same time introducing some new aspects of Jewish practice and activity which were judged to be inappropriate for examination by younger pupils.

JUDAISM

Along with its set of practices, Judaism also involves a sophisticated set of beliefs, spiritual insights and experiences. These in turn bear a complex relationship to general human experience and to the experience of pupils in particular.

EXAMPLE TOPICS

The maturing of pupils' interests and abilities allows for a richer diet of educational experiences. Quite extensive work on Jewish beliefs and spirituality can now be linked to work on Jewish influence on public life. A direct study of the relationship between Jewish faith and shared human experience can also be part of the programme for upper secondary pupils.

FUTURE WORK

It is hoped that work done with these pupils will provide a summation of their R.E. learning. Some will go on to take examinations. Some may find work which draws on the knowledge and insights gained from this subject. All will participate in life's joys, challenges, disappointments and mystery.

Area of study: *Jews in public life*

The ethical precepts and teachings of Judaism have a major effect on the way Jews participate in public life. Justice is one of the strongest values of Jewish ethics, and the attempt to bring about justice in society is, for many Jews, a central goal.

In considering the topic of Jews in public life it is helpful to remember that Jews live all over the world under different governmental structures and in different social climates. So, there cannot be a uniform way of dealing with matters of justice – each situation demands a different response.

This unit suggests three topics which may help upper secondary students to examine Jewish public life as it confronts various issues and situations. The first is designed to help pupils explore some Jewish attitudes towards social issues such as ecology, racism and war and peace. The second and third deal with matters that specifically and particularly affect Jews, the Holocaust and the state of Israel.

Topic: Attitudes to social issues
  (a) Jews and ecology
  (b) Jews and racism
  (c) War and peace

Topic: The Holocaust
  (a) Biblical accounts of persecution
  (b) Anti-Semitism in Eastern Europe
  (c) The extermination of Jews
  (d) Remembering the Holocaust

Topic: The state of Israel
  (a) Law of Return
  (b) Zionism
  (c) Soviet Jewry

The topic worked out as a sample unit of work is 'The Holocaust'.

Content overview

Hatred of Jews has a long history stretching back to biblical accounts of anti-Judaism in Maccabees and the book of Esther. *Ḥanukkah* and *Purim* both commemorate historical events when outside forces attempted to destroy Jews and Judaism.

From ancient times Jews have been made scapegoats and forced to take the blame on behalf of others for many things that went wrong. In the Middle Ages, Jews were blamed for the death of Jesus. Throughout history Jews have been denied religious freedom and have often had to live and trade in restricted areas. In the Soviet Union Jews have had their religious freedom restricted and have seldom been allowed to emigrate to Israel.

In many of these historical examples, Jews have been persecuted because of their religion. The 20th century has seen much pressure on Jews to become 'like everyone else' by assimilation. Assimilation is an English word for the Hebrew concept of 'imitating the nations' – behaving like 'everyone else'.

Anti-Semitism in Nazi Germany was based not only on religion, however, but on false notions of Jews as a race that threatened to take over important agencies such as the professions and centres of learning. They were also accused of being in league with communists.

It is important that pupils come to see the events of the Second World War in the context of this long history of persecution and denial of religious freedom. The activity in which the pupils imagine what it was like to celebrate *Pesaḥ* in a concentration camp may be especially helpful in doing this. Here, questions may be raised regarding the importance of Jewish identity and freedom under the threat of ultimate oppression.

Today, some Jews commemorate the atrocities of the Holocaust on *Yom HaShoah* (Holocaust Day) which falls on the 27th of *Nisan*. On this day Jews reaffirm their opposition to all tyranny and prejudice. *Yom HaShoah* is not observed by all Jews because of a desire not to add another day of mourning to the Jewish calendar. Some Jews prefer, therefore, to remember the victims of the Holocaust at *Tisha b'Av*, a day of mourning for many tragedies throughout Jewish history. Another way of keeping alive the memory of this terrible time in history is by visiting Yad Vashem, a memorial in Israel to the victims of the Holocaust.

This unit is also designed to elicit questions about prejudice and its consequences. Pupils should be encouraged to reflect on their own attitudes to prejudice. Questions to raise may include, 'Should we respect everyone?', 'Could I do this?', 'Could it happen here?'

The importance of commemoration and remembrance can be explored in order that pupils may reflect on the question, 'How do we ensure "never again"?'

Aims

Knowing:

1 some examples of persecution throughout Jewish history
2 some details of persecution of the Jews by the Nazis.

Understanding:

1 the importance of religious identity and freedom
2 some of the ways people responded to the persecution of Jews by the Nazis
3 the meaning of terms such as anti-Semitism and assimilation.

Reflecting on:

1 pupils' own attitudes to prejudice and oppression
2 the application of moral principles to issues of the Holocaust
3 the importance of commemoration and remembrance.

Activities

The following activities are some examples of work which can be undertaken to achieve the aims of this particular unit across the upper secondary range. It is left to teachers' professional judgement to select, amend, add to and sequence learning activities which suit their particular situations.

- Split the class in half and ask one group to examine the book of Esther and the other group the first and second books of Maccabees. Encourage each group to look for the particular reasons behind the persecution and the reaction of the Jews in each event. Encourage the two groups to come together and discuss the similarities and differences in the way in which the Jewish community reacted, and the form the persecution took.

- Invite a survivor of the Holocaust, or a descendant or relative of a Holocaust survivor, into the classroom. If such a person is not available, tapes of survivors may be useful or a book such as Elie Wiesel's *Night*. Encourage the class to explore the effect the Holocaust had on the individual and his or her family, looking especially at the ongoing consequences to the family.

- Encourage the class to research various non-Jewish responses to the Holocaust. Discuss the possible motives and feelings of (1) those who opposed what was happening to the Jews; (2) those who knew about the concentration camps but said and did nothing; and (3) those who supported the mass killings.

- Read out some examples of poetry or auto-biography (e.g. Anne Frank) or show some examples of Jewish art from the period of the Holocaust. Help the pupils to explore the feelings expressed in these works. Then help the class to identify beliefs or values expressed in these works that may have helped the Jews through their experiences.

- Ask the pupils to read the section in *Jews* 4 on the Hall of Names at Yad Vashem, the Holocaust memorial in Israel. Encourage the pupils to discuss the importance of remembrance. They might consider the following: Is 'remembering' enough to make sure such a thing will not happen again? Is remembrance of such horror just ghoulish?

- Help the pupils to write and stage a drama with one of these scenarios.

(a) A Jewish family living in England at the time of the Holocaust are celebrating *Pesah*. They have relatives in Germany. Encourage the pupils to bring out the feelings the family might have and the parallels with the events leading up to the Exodus.

(b) *Pesah* is being celebrated in a concentration camp. Encourage the pupils to bring out how the Jews might feel about those who have already perished and about their families who might be in other concentration camps or safe in other countries.

- Give the class the statement, 'Where was God?' Distribute copies of *Jews* 4 and ask the pupils to read the section on God in the part on 'Jewish beliefs'. Split the class into three and ask each group to take one of the responses to suffering stated in *Jews 4*: (1) God's response to Job; (2) God is dead after Auschwitz; (3) free will must allow evil human actions, and to write a short (200-word) discussion paper enlarging on this point of view. Ask each group to present their paper to the full class.

- Encourage the class to research examples of responses to suffering from biblical texts, e.g. Job 30: 9–31 and God's response in Job 38: 2–21. Ask the pupils to imagine themselves in the place of Job and the reaction they might have to God's response.

Area of study: *Jewish community life*

The central concept of this unit is the worldwide Jewish community, the allegiance most Jews feel to other Jews, no matter where they live or the exact way they practise their religion.

In some sense, this worldwide Jewish community is held together by bonds of common experience. The first topic enables pupils to look at the way in which the larger Jewish community can be said to share a history, a language and a land and how this sharing contributes to a unity which has survived the many forces which might have torn it apart. The second topic explores the diversity, geographical and ideological, which exists within that unity.

Topic: The Jewish people
  (a) A shared history
  (b) A shared language
  (c) A shared land

Topic: Jewish diversity
  (a) Geographical diversity – Sefardi and Ashkenazi

The topic worked out as a sample unit of work is 'Jewish diversity'.

Topic	Jewish diversity

Content overview
While it is important that pupils appreciate the unity of Jews as a people who share a history, a language and a land, it is important that they also appreciate that there are many differences between various sections of the world community of Jews.

Some of the differences result from geographical factors. In a religion as old as Judaism it is to be expected that communities separated from each other by geography should develop customs of their own.

The basic geographical division between Sefardi Jews (Oriental) and Ashkenazi Jews (Western) arose during the Middle Ages. The Sefardi tradition arose in Spain. Under Muslim rulers Spanish Jews enjoyed much prosperity and their influence spread to other communities in the Mediterranean. Many of them spoke a language called Ladino, a form of Spanish, as well as Hebrew. *Ashkenazi* is the Hebrew word used for Germany. In the Middle Ages, large sections of the Jewish community of Germany were forced out by persecutions that followed the Crusades and the Black Death. They went to countries such as Poland, Lithuania, Russia and northern France but, like the Sefardi Jews, kept many customs in common. They spoke Yiddish, a form of German.

Arising out of this geographical division are variations of custom ranging from different ways of pronouncing Hebrew to differences in styles of graves, the Sefardi Jews using flat gravestones and the Ashkenazi using stones that are raised at the head. The majority of Jews in England are now Ashkenazi Jews.

Differences within Judaism are not just geographical. There are also ideological differences based on the understanding of the nature of revelation and the associated question of authority.

The broad divisions are Orthodox and Progressive. Briefly, Orthodox Jews believe that the *Torah* is a direct revelation of the word of God and that the teachings of the rabbis are part of this unbroken chain of authority.

Progressive Jews accept that the *Torah* is divinely inspired but say that, as it was written down by human beings at different times, certain elements of it may not be directly applicable to contemporary Jewish life. There are, of course, other less fundamental but significant differences between these two broad traditions.

It is important that pupils do not stereotype members of religious traditions. Hence the importance of understanding that Jews do not all think alike nor follow the same practices.

Aims

Knowing:
1 the basic geographical division between Sefardi and Ashkenazi Jews
2 some of the ideological differences between Orthodox and Progressive Jews

3 some of the divisions both within Orthodox and within Progressive Judaism and some of the differences in their belief and practice.

Understanding:
1 that different beliefs about 'authority' have played and continue to play a significant role in the diversity within Judaism
2 that amongst Jews there is disagreement about the value of diversity in belief and practice
3 that differences in custom do not necessarily point to differences in belief.

Reflecting on:
1 the belief that diversity is to be welcomed and enjoyed
2 the belief that God's self-revelation is through particular events and people and that in Orthodox belief, the authority of such revelation is not to be questioned
3 the Progressive belief that in matters of religion, the authority of personal conscience and experience is paramount.

Activities

The following activities are some examples of work which can be undertaken to achieve the aims of this particular unit across the upper secondary range. It is left to teachers' professional judgement to select, amend, add to and sequence learning activities which suit their particular situations.

- Encourage the class to enact a situation depicting different authority figures and responses to a particular problem, e.g. a 14-year-old girl has a drug problem and is being advised by a panel made up of a police officer, parent, headteacher, doctor, social worker and another 14-year-old. Encourage the class to explore what sort of authority each of the panel exercises.
- Ask the class to discuss the following: 'Who or what influences what I wear to . . . a wedding, a funeral, school, a party, etc.' Explore with the class how their choices are influenced and by whom.
- Encourage the pupils to research the history and development of the Falasha Jews, particularly exploring the question of whether this group can maintain its own distinct identity while learning to live as part of the wider Jewish community.
- Split the class into two groups and give each group one of the following statements: 'Cultural diversity enriches British society and should be encouraged'; 'Cultural diversity is divisive and destructive to British society'. Ask each group to

prepare a short presentation, including 'evidence' to back up their point, and present this to the whole class.

- (a) Ask two pupils to read out the dialogue between Judith and David in the section, 'Community life' in *Jews 4*. Encourage the pupils to explore the reasons for the differences in Jewish food traditions between the Ashkenazi and the Sefardi communities. Using a Jewish cookbook, encourage the pupils to find different recipes which are traditional in the different community, e.g. latkes (Ashkenazi) and dfeena (Sefardi).

  (b) Discuss with the class what is so essential to Judaism that it has not been changed by cultural, historical or geographical factors.

Encourage the pupils to look at prayers such as the *Shema* and *Amidah.*

- Distribute copies of *Jews 4* and copies of a topographical world map. Using the world map showing different Jewish communities in *Jews 4*, explore possible routes that may have been taken from Germany and from Spain to where Jewish communities settled. Ask the pupils to use different colours for the routes of the two groups.

- Using two English dialects (e.g. Geordie and Cornish) ask the class to explore how these dialects evolved within the same country. Encourage the pupils to look at geographical and historical reasons why dialects develop.

Area of study: *Jewish spirituality*

Spirituality in Judaism is not an easy topic. Although it has been dealt with indirectly in previous units, upper secondary pupils will perhaps find investigating it in some depth more rewarding than younger pupils.

The spirituality of Judaism translates the commandments of *Torah*, in which God's presence is reflected, into the actions of life. In other words, right actions are carried out in response to God's will and commandments. Humanity and God work together in the world to fulfil the divine intention for the universe.

The first topic in this unit deals with religious experience in Judaism. The *Halakhah* is the spiritual path, in the form of laws, which connects *Torah* to action. The attempt to follow this path results in the spiritual experiences of daily life, the next aspect of this topic. Thirdly, the mystic strand in Judaism, the *Kabbalah,* is considered. Pupils are

introduced to some of the basic ideas of Jewish mysticism – for example, the notion that the process of the creation of the universe resulted in disunity in the universe which humanity is called upon to repair.

The second topic is intended to help upper secondary pupils to learn something about the values that are a part of Jewish spirituality.

Topic: Religious experience
(a) *Halakhah* – a way, path
(b) Spiritual experiences in daily life
(c) *Kabbalah* – mysticism

Topic: Jewish values
(a) Love
(b) Justice and mercy
(c) Holiness

The topic worked out as a sample unit of work is 'Jewish values'.

Topic	Jewish values

Content overview
Ideas of Jewish spirituality have been implied in most of the work done on this religion throughout the primary and lower secondary years.

Like all religions, certain beliefs and values lie at the core of Judaism. It is an important job of the teacher, throughout a pupil's schooling, to be aware of the importance of Jewish spirituality and to perceive the connections between it and Jewish practice.

Jewish spirituality is the spirituality of the *Halakhah*. This means attempting to carry out the word of God and perceive the will of God as it has been revealed in the *Torah*.

This unit focuses on Jewish values that in some way reflect Jewish ideas about the nature of God. Through living the life of *Torah* human beings are supposed, as far as possible, to take on some of the characteristics of God and thus transmit the written word of *Torah* into action in the world.

Three important values are central to Jewish spirituality. The first is love and compassion. Jews believe that the *Torah* has been given in love and is fulfilled in love. The ideal of love extends to all human beings as expressed in the commandment that 'you shall love your fellow as yourself' (Leviticus 19: 18).

Secondly, the literal meaning of the Hebrew term used for charity – *tzedeḵah* – is justice. Justice in this sense includes the just distribution of resources as well as legal justice and just dealing in business. Much of *Halakhah* is devoted to the establishment of a just society and therefore to the inculcation of the ideal of justice.

Thirdly, holiness is a central value. The Hebrew word *ḵedusha* is derived from a root meaning 'set apart'. The quality of holiness flows from God who is greater than anything humanity can comprehend.

Holiness is encountered in all aspects of Jewish living. Examples found in the 19th chapter of Leviticus illustrate a way of making ordinary and everyday things and events sacred. Eating is a particular example of this. By following the requirements of the food laws, a basic physical act becomes something holy, a form of religious expression.

Aims

Knowing:
1 at least one of the values believed to be central to Jewish spirituality, e.g. love, justice, holiness
2 some examples of Jewish teaching which stress the importance of particular values and recognise examples of Jewish practice by which they can be identified
3 how objects found in a Jewish home can express holiness in daily life.

Understanding:
1 that Jewish spirituality is implicit in the obligations and duties that are imposed upon Jews by the covenant relationship with God
2 how Jewish values derive from the meaning of *Halakhah*
3 that Jewish values have not only spiritual but practical applications.

Reflecting on:
1 the belief that human beings, as far as possible, should take on the attributes of God
2 the value of transcendental ideas and idealistic visions of human character
3 pupils' own beliefs as to what are important values in life.

Activities

The following activities are some examples of work which can be undertaken to achieve the aims of this particular unit across the upper secondary range. It is left to teachers' professional judgement to select, amend, add to and sequence learning activities which suit their particular situations.

- Divide the class into two parts and organise a debate on the topic: 'To give money to the poor is not charity but merely to act justly'.

- Divide the class into small groups to explore their own personal ideas of what makes a 'just' society and what steps they would see as necessary to change their present society into a just one.

- Distribute copies of Leviticus 19. Encourage the class to explore the rules it contains. Help the class to consider in what way these rules might be relevant to contemporary Jewish life.

- (a) Read Leviticus 19: 9 and 23–25 with the class. These verses give laws regarding crops and harvesting. Discuss the practical advantages of following the laws, e.g. verse 9 – a way of helping the poor; verses 23–25 – giving the crops time to mature so that there will be a better harvest.

  (b) Using the verses given above, explore the reasons why these practical rules are regarded as holy, i.e. bringing God into all aspects of life, doing what is commanded in the *Torah*.

  (c) Ask the class to notice the repetition of the 'I am the Lord your God' in Leviticus 19, and ask them to consider the effect this has on the reader.

- Show a *mezuzah* to the class and discuss its use and role in the family home. Encourage the class to read and consider the *mitzvah* to which it relates (Deuteronomy 11: 18–21). Ask them to explore the question of whether all *mitzvot* have 'practical reasons' behind them, and if not, why God commands them to be done.

- Organise the class into two groups. Give one group the sentence, 'Acting in a "loving" way towards someone you don't like is hypocritical' and the sentence 'Acting in a "loving" way towards someone you don't like will cause "love" to grow'. Encourage the two groups to debate these statements, each pressing their given point.

Area of study: *Jewish beliefs*

Judaism is not a dogmatic religion in the sense that it does not expect its adherents to accept an agreed list of beliefs. At this stage of schooling, pupils should have an appreciation of the fact that Jews do not all share the same views. Also, they should be aware that for many Jews concrete practices are of the utmost importance in the following of their religion.

However, behind these practices lies a variety of beliefs that enable Jews not only to live their lives in the world but help them answer some of the puzzling and disturbing questions that all human beings face. Whilst for many Jews action is as important as belief, action is empty and meaningless without underlying beliefs and spirituality.

Topic: Principal Jewish beliefs
(a) God
(b) Covenant
(c) *Torah*
(d) The People of Israel
(e) Free will and human nature
(f) Repentance
(g) Messiah and redemption

This topic is worked out as a sample scheme of work.

Topic	Principal Jewish beliefs

Content overview

Although Judaism is not a religion which has a creed or formal statement of beliefs, most Jewish people who are committed to Judaism would appeal to beliefs about God, covenant, *Torah*, commandment, Israel, human nature and free will, repentance and Messiah. Whilst Jews may disagree about the emphasis given to each of these beliefs, these eight concepts form the basis of the Jewish understanding of the meaning and purpose of life.

It is important to remember that pupils entering upper secondary classes may well bring with them a variety of understandings and misunderstandings of these areas of Jewish belief. Those who have had a regular and sustained religious education may have explored them in an indirect way.

Now, however, pupils are expected to consider these beliefs in a direct way. They should also be helped to see some ways in which these beliefs link with important areas of shared human experience and questioning. For discussion on the nature of these links, see *How do I teach R.E?* and Part One of this manual.

Aims

Knowing:
1 in general outline, some of the key beliefs which Jews hold about God, Covenant, *Torah*, commandment, Israel, human nature, repentance and Messiah
2 some of the foundations for Jewish beliefs; e.g. *Torah* and the oral tradition (*Mishnah* and *Talmud*)

3 some of the ways in which several key areas of Jewish belief relate to significant areas of shared human experience.

Understanding:
1 that Jewish beliefs are expressed through a variety of practices and cannot be fully appreciated without reference to these practices
2 that Jews differ as to the emphasis they place on various beliefs
3 that different Jewish movements hold different views about the authority of *Torah, Mishnah* and *Talmud,* etc.

Reflecting on:
1 the value of using a framework of religious beliefs as one way of asserting self-identity and personal goals and commitments
2 the extent to which pupils themselves relate to any or all of these areas of Jewish belief
3 the links between religious beliefs and moral behaviour.

Activities

The following activities are some examples of work which can be undertaken to achieve the aims of this particular unit across the upper secondary range. It is left to teachers' professional judgement to select, amend, add to and sequence learning activities which suit their particular situations.

● Show picture 7 of *Sefer Torah* from *Jews Photopack* to the class and ask the pupils to look at the section on *Torah*. Using the text and the picture, discuss the different ways in which respect is shown and importance given to the *Torah*.

- Encourage the pupils to design a chart or diagram to highlight the differences between Orthodox and Progressive beliefs about how *Torah* expresses the word of God. Discuss with the class how both Progressive and Orthodox Jews believe that the *Torah* is communication from God but see its authority in different ways.

- Ask the class to brainstorm the word 'God' to make a list of the ways in which pupils understand the concept. Read to the class the different quotations about the nature of God from this manual (pp. 5–8), and discuss any similarities and differences between the perception of the class and the qualities of God expressed in the quotations.

- Ask the class to read psalms expressing praise to God (e.g. Psalms 27, 29, 33, 34, 47). Using these psalms explore with the class what it is about God that evokes such praise. Encourage the pupils to think about why praising God is such an important part of Jewish religious practice.

- Distribute copies of *Jews 4* to three pupils and ask them to read out the dialogue on *shehitah* (slaughter). Show the class the picture from *Jews Photopack* on *kashrut* and read out the information on the back. Encourage the pupils to discuss how religious beliefs are expressed in the activities of daily life, such as preparing and eating meals.

- Read from *Jews 4* the second paragraph in the section on God in the part called 'Jewish beliefs' (on ethical monotheism). Ask the pupils to read the section 'Jews and the issue of ecology' in the part on 'Jews and public life'. Discuss with the pupils what specific aspects of Jewish belief lead the author to suggest that a Jewish contribution 'to thought on ecological issues would be beneficial'.

- Ask the pupils to read the section in *Jews 4* 'The People of Israel' in the part on 'Jewish beliefs'. Encourage the pupils to consider the Orthodox definition of being Jewish and to speculate on why the mother's Jewishness is the criterion. What are some different ways to determine 'birth' and lineage?

Select bibliography

Basic texts

Tanakh (Hebrew Bible) English translation from Jewish Publication Society, 1985

Mishnah English translation by Danby, H., Oxford University Press, 1963

Siddur (prayer book)

Orthodox: *Authorised Daily Prayer Book*, Eyre & Spottiswode, 1962

Reform: *Forms of Prayer*, Reform Synagogues of Great Britain, 1977

Liberal: *Service of the Heart*, Union of Liberal and Progressive Synagogues, 1967

Reference

Roth, Cecil (ed) *Encyclopaedia Judaica*, Keter, 1972

Wood, Angela *Dictionaries of World Religions: Judaism*, Batsford Educational, 1984

Cole, W. Owen and Morgan, Peggy *Six Religions in the Twentieth Century*, Hulton Educational, 1984

General books

Alexander, Philip *Textual Sources for the Study of Judaism*, Manchester University Press, 1984

Blue, Lionel *To Heaven with Scribes and Pharisees*, Darton, Longman and Todd, 1975

Donan, Hayyim H. *To Be a Jew*, Basic Books, 1972

Epstein, Isidore *Judaism*, Pelican Books, 1959

Forta, Arye *Examining Religions: Judaism*, Heinemann Educational, 1989

Greenberg, Blu *How to Run a Traditional Jewish Household*, Simon and Schuster, 1983

Holtz, Barry *Back to the Sources*, Summit Books, 1984

Jacobs, Louis *The Book of Jewish Belief*, Behrman House, 1984

United Reformed Church *Christians and Jews in Britain*, U.R.C., 1983

Unterman, Alan *Jews, their Beliefs and Practices*, Routledge and Kegan Paul, 1981

History

Dawidowicz, Lucy *The War Against the Jews, 1933–1945*, Penguin, 1975

Gilbert, Martin *The Jewish History Atlas*, Weidenfeld and Nicholson, 1976

Laqueur, Walter *The History of Zionism*, Holt, Rhinehart and Winston, 1972

Margolis, Max and Marx, A. *History of the Jewish People*, Jewish Publication Society, 1964

Polack, A. and Lawrence, J. *The Cup of Life*, S.P.C.K., 1976

Sachar, Howard M. *The Course of Modern Jewish History*, World, 1958

Special topics

Berkovits, Eliezer *Not in Heaven, the nature & function of Halakha*, Ktav, 1983

Greenberg, Blu *On Women and Judaism*, Jewish Publication Society, 1981

Neusner, Jacob *Understanding Rabbinic Judaism*, Ktav, 1974

Scholem, Gershom *Major Trends in Jewish Mysticism*, Schocken, 1965

Glossary

Readers are advised to refer to the short section on the transliteration of Hebrew words on page vi.

'adam   Hebrew for 'humanity' c.f. Genesis 1: 27
'God created *adam* in his own image, in the image of God he created him, male and female he created them.'

'afikoman   the portion of *matzah* eaten at the end of the *Seder* as a reminder of the Paschal sacrifice

'Akdamut   Aramaic hymns glorifying God and *Torah* sung at *Shavuot*

'Akedah   (lit. 'binding') c.f. Genesis 22, the account of the binding of Isaac; read at *Rosh haShanah* services and as part of morning prayer

'Alenu   (lit. 'it is our duty . . .') first word of concluding prayer of all services, referring to hope for ultimate salvation

'Al-Het   (lit. 'for the sin of . . .') alphabetical confession of sins, mostly ethical, recited at *Yom Kippur* services

'Aliyah   (lit. 'going up') (a) being called to the public reading of the *Torah* at synagogue services; (b) emigration to Israel

'Amidah   (lit. 'standing') the central part of every prayer service consisting of 19 blessings recited while standing

Aramaic   Semitic language, used as vernacular in ancient Palestine and Babylon

'arba'ah kanfot   see *tallit katan*

'Arba'ah Minim   the four species held for part of *Sukkot* service: citron, palm, willow and myrtle

'Aron HaKodesh   (lit. 'holy ark') the cupboard in the eastern wall of the synagogue in which the scrolls of *Torah* are kept

Ashkenaz   Hebrew for Germany, also used of Jewish communities of northern, central and eastern Europe

'Avodah   (lit. 'work') divine service, particularly Temple service

B.C.E.   Before the Common Era; used instead of B.C. (Before Christ)

Ba'al Teshuvah   a penitent, especially one of non-religious background who has returned to traditional observance

Bar/Bat Mitzvah   (lit. 'son/daughter of the commandment') denotes the transition to adult status of the 13-year-old boy/12-year-old girl

berakhah   blessing, prayer using formula 'Blessed are you, Lord our God, King of the universe . . .'

Bet Knesset   house of meeting ⎫
Bet Midrash   house of study ⎬ designations for the synagogue
Bet Tefillah   house of prayer ⎭

bimah   platform in synagogue from which *Torah* is read

Birkat haMazon   grace after meals

brit   covenant, a relationship of mutual love and responsibility between God and humanity

Brit Milah   covenant of circumcision, the sign of the covenant between God and Abraham

C.E.   Common Era; used by non-Christians instead of A.D. (Anno Domini, year of our Lord)

Conservative   American movement, non-fundamentalist in outlook but fairly traditional in practice

Diaspora   (lit. 'scattering') Greek word used for dispersion of Jews to countries outside Israel

dukhan   (lit. 'platform') practice of priests blessing the people, c.f. Numbers 6: 22–26

etrog   citron, one of the *Arba'ah Minim*

Gemara   (lit. 'completion') record of debates of rabbis on *Mishnah* compiled c.500 C.E.

Gematria   exegetical tradition using numerical values of Hebrew letters and words

Gemilut Hasadim   (lit. 'loving deeds') used of interpersonal practical compassion

get   divorce document

Haftarah   (lit. 'completion') prophetical portion chanted or read after reading of *Torah* in synagogue on *Shabbat*

Hagaddah   (lit. 'telling') book used in re-telling of Exodus story at the *Seder* meal on the first evening of *Pesah*

Halakhah   (lit. 'the way') the legal teachings of traditional Judaism

Hallah   loaves used on Sabbath and festivals

Hametz   leaven, anything made of grain; forbidden during whole week of *Pesah*

Hanukkah   (lit. 'dedication') holiday celebrating the rededication of the Temple in the time of the Maccabbees, 165 B.C.E.; usually occurring in December

haOlam haBa   the world to come, the time of redemption

Hasid   (lit. 'pious one') member of the hasidic sect, founded in the 18th century in eastern Europe, emphasising joyous worship and mystical relationship with God

Havdalah   (lit. 'separation') ceremony marking the end of the Sabbath and festivals, made over wine, spices and the light of a plaited candle

hazzan   cantor, person who leads prayer using traditional tunes

Hevra Kadisha   (lit. 'holy group') people who care for body after burial, performing *Taharah* and watching over body

Hiddur Mitzvah   (lit. 'adornment of *mitzvah*') performing *mitzvah* in the most beautiful way possible

Hol haMoed   festive weekdays, the days of *Pesah* and *Sukkot* between the festival days at beginning and end

Holocaust   genocide of 6,000,000 Jews under the Nazi regime in Second World War

Hoshana Rabba   last day of *Hol HaMoed Sukkot*, marked by prayer for water and chanting of hymns with refrain *Hosha'na*, 'save us'

huppah   canopy used in wedding ceremony to symbolise couple's new home

Kabbalah   Jewish mystical tradition

Kaddish   Aramaic prayer praising God, used to mark end of section of the service; also recited by mourners

Karaites   group originating in the eighth century C.E. who did not accept oral *Torah*

kasher   (lit. 'fit, proper') used of food fit to eat according to dietary laws

kashrut   derived from *kasher*; used of dietary laws

kavannah   (lit. 'intention') internal awareness of spiritual meaning of performance of *mitzvot*

Kedusha   prayer declaring holiness of God (Isaiah 6: 3) recited as part of *Amidah*

ketuba   wedding document, detailing rights of wife

Ketuvim   (lit. 'Writings') last section of Bible, including Psalms, Proverbs

Kiddush   (lit. 'sanctification') prayer proclaiming holiness of Sabbath and festivals, recited before meals on those days over a cup of wine

kiddushin   (lit. 'sanctification') marriage

kippah   head covering worn by Jewish men

kittel   white garment (symbolising purity) worn by traditional Jews on *Yom Kippur*, *Seder* evening by celebrant, by bridegroom and as a shroud

kohen   priest, descendant of the priestly families

Kol Nidrei   (lit. 'all the vows') prayer which begins *Yom Kippur* services and hence name by which first service of *Yom Kippur* is known

Ladino   also called Judaeo-Spanish; vernacular of Sefardi Jews

Lag ba'Omer   33rd day of Omer; semi-festival, interrupting mourning of *Omer* period

Liberal   non-traditional movement, founded in England, 1902; less traditional than Reform

Limmud haTorah   study of *Torah*

liShmah   (lit. 'for its own sake') performance of *mitzvah* for its own sake, not for any possible material benefit

lulav   palm branch, one of *Arba'ah Minim*

Ma'ariv   evening prayers

Mahzor   (lit. 'cycle') prayer book used for festival prayers

mamzer   child born of a union that should never have taken place, e.g. adulterous, incestuous

Mashiah   (lit. 'anointed') the Messiah

matzah   (pl. *matzot*), the unleavened bread used on *Pesah*

megillah   (lit. 'scroll') used particularly of the five scrolls, Ruth, Song of Songs, Lamentation, Ecclesiastes, and especially of Esther, read on *Purim*

menorah   seven-branched candelabrum used in Temple

mezuzah   (lit. 'doorpost') parchment containing paragraphs of *Shema* fastened to doorposts in a Jewish home

Midrash   exegetical tradition expounding Bible, mostly from Talmudic period. *Midrash Aggada* concentrates on ethical material, *Midrash Halakha* on legal material

Mikdash Me'at   (lit. 'little sanctuary') sometimes used to refer to the home

mikveh   bath of natural rainwater, used by married women after their periods before sleeping with their husbands again, and by some men

minhag   custom, as opposed to *mitzvah*, commandment

Minhah   afternoon prayers

minyan   quorum of 10 adult males required for community prayer

Mishloah Manot   sending gifts to friends on *Purim*

Mishnah   first codification of oral law, completed c.200 C.E.

mitzvah   (lit. 'commandment'; pl. *mitzvot*) individual unit of law prescribed in *Torah*

Mizrah   a plaque found in some homes to indicate the direction of Jerusalem

mohel   someone trained to perform *Brit Milah*

Musaf   additional service, recited on *Shabbat* and festivals

Ner Tamid   the eternal light, found in many synagogues to remind people of God's eternal presence

Nevi'im   prophets, the second section of the Bible

Nusah   the traditional chants used for prayer in the synagogue

'Omer   (lit. 'sheaf') the 49-day period between *Pesah* and *Shavuot*

Orthodox   the traditional, fundamentalist movement in Judaism

parashah   the five books of Moses are divided into 54 *parshiyot* (pl.); one (sometimes two) *parashah* is read each Sabbath in the synagogue

parev   used of food that is neither meat nor milk and can therefore be eaten with either, e.g. vegetables, fish, eggs, fruit

Pesah   Passover, spring festival celebrating Exodus from Egypt

Pharisees   group who followed interpretations of oral *Torah* c.100 B.C.E. – 100 C.E.

Pidyon haBen   redemption of firstborn; ceremony redeeming firstborn son from Temple service, retained by Orthodox despite destruction of Temple

Progressive   blanket term used of all non-Orthodox movements in Judaism

Purim   holiday celebrating events described in book of Esther; occurring in February or March

rabbi   (lit. 'teacher') originally title of respect for any sage; now usually applied to any graduate from a rabbinical seminary

rahmanut   compassion

Reconstructionism   American non-traditional movement in Judaism

Reform   non-fundamentalist movement, less traditional than Conservative, more traditional than Liberal

Rosh haShanah   New Year festival, marked by sounding of *shofar* and initiating a period of repentance

Rosh Hodesh   the new moon, marking the beginning of each Jewish month; celebrated as a minor festival

Sadducees   group, contemporary with Pharisees, who followed written *Torah* only

sandek   man who holds baby for circumcision ceremony

Seder   (lit. 'order') first evening of *Pesah* when Exodus story is retold

Sefardi   Hebrew for Spain, also used for Jewish communities from entire Mediterranean area

sefer Torah   scroll of *Torah*; handwritten version of five books of Moses written on parchment

Selihot   penitential prayers, held from before *Rosh haShanah* to *Yom Kippur*

Se'udat Mitzvah   meal eaten to celebrate a *mitzvah*, e.g. circumcision, wedding, *Bar/Bat Mitzvah*

Shabbat   the Sabbath, celebrated from Friday sunset to Saturday evening

Shaharit   the morning prayers

shalom   Hebrew for peace

Shalosh Regalim   the three pilgrim festivals, *Pesah*, *Shavuot*, *Sukkot*

Shavuot   (lit. 'weeks') festival of revelation of *Torah*, seven weeks after *Pesah*

shehitah   slaughter performed according to Jewish law

Shekhinah   God's presence, the immanent side of God

Sheloshim   (lit. 'thirty') month of mourning following a burial

Shema   (lit. 'hear') first word of Deuteronomy 6: 4, 'Hear O Israel, the Lord our God, the Lord is one'. This proclamation of God's unity is recited twice daily.

Shemini Atzeret   eighth day of Solemn Assembly, festival celebrated as last day of *Sukkot*

Sheva Berakhot   the seven blessings recited at a wedding; by extension, feasts held for the bridal couple for the week after the wedding

Sheva Mitzvot B'nei Noah   the seven commandments of Noah's descendants, which Jews believe all humanity should keep

Shemoneh Esre   (lit. 'eighteen') the '*Amidah* which is made up of 19, originally 18, blessings

shiur   study session

Shiva   (lit. 'seven') first period of intense mourning, lasting a week after the burial

Shiviti   plaque with God's name on it, to remind us of God's presence (c.f. Psalm 16: 8)

shofar   ram's horn trumpet, used on *Rosh haShanah*

Shohet   one trained to carry out *shehitah*

shul   Yiddish for synagogue

Shulhan Arukh   (lit. 'prepared table') most famous code of Jewish law, compiled c.1550 C.E.

Siddur   (lit. 'arrangement, order') Jewish prayer book

Simhat Torah   rejoicing of the *Torah*; last day of *Shemini Atzeret*

sukkah   booth or hut built for the celebration of *Sukkot*

Sukkot   (lit. 'huts') festival celebrating harvest and the desert wanderings of the Israelites after the Exodus, occuring in September or October

taharah   purification, washing of dead body for burial

Taharat haMishpahah   (lit. 'family purity') laws governing marital relations at time of woman's period

tallit   prayer shawl worn at daily morning prayer by the adult male

tallit katan   small version of above worn all day by Orthodox males; also called '*arba'ah kanfot* (lit. 'four corners')

Talmud   combination of *Mishnah* and *Gemara*, one version from Babylon and one from Palestine

Tanakh   Bible, an acronym made up of *Torah*, *Nevi'im*, *Ketuvim*

Tashlikh   ceremony performed on afternoon of *Rosh haShanah*, symbolically casting sins into water

tefillah   prayer

tefillin   phylacteries, leather boxes on straps containing passages from *Torah*, worn at morning prayer (not on Sabbath) by adult male

Tena'im   betrothal ceremony

teshuvah   (lit. 'returning') repentance

Tikkun leil Shavuot   all-night study session held on *Shavuot*

Tisha b'Av   ninth day of *Av*, fast commemorating destruction of Temple

Torah   (lit. 'teaching, instruction') narrow sense: the five books of Moses (*Torah she bikhtav*: written *Torah*); broad sense: the whole of traditional Jewish teaching (*Torah she b'al peh*: oral *Torah*)

trefa   (lit. 'torn') food that has not been prepared according to dietary laws

Tu biSh'vat   15th day of *Sh'vat*, New Year for Trees

tzedakah   (lit. 'justice') charity

tzitzit   fringes attached to *tallit*, c.f. Numbers 15: 37–40

Viddui   confession recited on *Yom Kippur*, before wedding by bridal couple and on death bed

yad   (lit. 'hand') pointer used in reading *Sefer Torah* to avoid touching and damaging parchment

yahrzeit   Yiddish for anniversary, especially of a death

yarmulke   Russian Yiddish for *kippah*

yeshiva   institute of higher Talmudic learning

Yetzer haTov, Yetzer haRa   the good and the evil inclinations

Yiddish   the vernacular of *Ashkenazi* Jews

Yizkor   memorial prayer recited on last day of pilgrim festivals and *Yom Kippur*

Yom ha'Atzma'ut   Israeli Independence Day (14th May, 1948)

Yom haShoah   Holocaust Remembrance Day

Yom Kippur   Day of Atonement, the culmination of 10 days of penitence initiated by *Rosh haShanah*; kept as a fast day

Yom Yerushalayim   day celebrating re-unification of Jerusalem (June 1967)

zemirot   Sabbath table songs

Zionism   movement supporting resettlement of and return of Jews to land of Israel

Index